THE 6IXTH EVOLUTION

Managing Lives and Careers Through Convulsive Times

DR. LARRY G. STRAUB

FIRST EDITION

Archway Publishing books may be ordered through booksellers or by contacting:

Archway Publishing
1663 Liberty Drive
Bloomington, IN 47403
www.archwaypublishing.com
844-669-3957

ISBN: 978-1-6657-1480-8 (sc)
ISBN: 978-1-6657-1479-2 (hc)
ISBN: 978-1-6657-1481-5 (e)

Library of Congress Control Number: 2021922651

Print information available on the last page.

Archway Publishing rev. date: 01/21/2022

CONTENTS

THE FIRST CONVULSION: THE FAMILY BUSINESS

PART 1: The Five Evolutions

THE SECOND CONVULSION: OUT OF THE FRYING PAN AND INTO THE FIRE

PART 2: The 6ixth Evolution: Living in an Age of Exponential Change and Hyper convulsive Environments

THE THIRD CONVULSION: INDUSTRY CONSOLIDATION AND "THE DEAL"

PART 3: The Promethean Framework: How to Position for Sustainability and Success in Convulsive Environments

THE FOURTH CONVULSION: RAPID GROWTH, THE NEXT GENS, AND "RIDING THE DRAGON"

PART 4: Welcome to 6e Thinking

THE FIFTH CONVULSION: THE SALE OF THE BUSINESS AND WHAT'S NEXT?

THE SIXTH CONVULSION: REINVENTION— NEW PATHWAYS AND NEW BEGINNINGS

AUTHOR NOTE

You will note that this book is labeled as the *first edition*. I see it as a work in progress that will have hopefully different editions after this one. Over the next couple of decades, I plan to learn with all of you about this intriguing and dynamic topic. It is my wish to encourage anyone and everyone who reads this to contribute to this dynamic, important, and quickly evolving topic.

This is just the start of a process that I hope will involve many others in decades of discovery. I don't intend to or pretend to be an expert on this subject, just a repository of data and a facilitator of grounded and developing knowledge. You can take part in this process by visiting my website at **http://larrystraub.com/** and leaving your comments and observations, as well as by taking the Promethean Framework Measurement Instrument survey.

Please feel free to utilize and share this manuscript. All I ask is that you do it with the intent it was designed for: to teach and educate people on how to position their lives and careers for the convulsive and dynamic environments that lie ahead.

I look forward to partnering and collaborating with anyone who has interest. Please reach out to me via the website listed above.

Regards,
Larry Straub

ACKNOWLEDGEMENTS

Writing acknowledgements can be tricky, there can and usually are so many that had an impact on your life, career as well as the events that led to the production of a work such as this. But it is always a fitting place to start with family.

My family acknowledgements take three distinct forms. First, my wife Julie, who has indulged and tolerated my evolving gyrations through our 36 year marriage, from business executive to professor to author. Without her love and support none of this would have been possible. Also to my children Hillary and Brantley, they have listened patiently and engaged in deliberations about many of these concepts and theories through the years.

Also, I owe a debt of gratitude to my family that worked with me at Straub International, Inc. We had an incredible journey together through these past years and much of what I am and have accomplished is because of their support and encouragement. Particular thanks to Ron and Kathy Straub for their backing of my educational endeavors through the years, this book is a direct offshoot of my doctoral level studies and dissertation.

A note of thanks as well to the remainder of my family.

Again… many of you have indulged in my conversations and rantings as well. While it may have been tedious at times, you always listened and contributed, helping me form and formalize my thoughts and ideas.

I would also offer a posthumous thank you to my late father Wally Straub. His encouragement of my growth through the years was invaluable, both in regards to business as well as intellectual pursuits. I offer this book in part as a testament to the life of this wonderful, brilliant and generous man.

A special thanks to Dr. Paul Hedlund and Dr. Phil Cola, two friends and fellow academics who were very supportive of me as I proceeded with this intellectual journey. Helping proof and theorize throughout the writing of my dissertation as well as this particular work.

Additionally, an acknowledgement to Dr. James Gaskin (Brigham Young University) and Dr. Peter Whitehouse (Case Western Reserve University) who both served as part of my Dissertation team and provided immeasurable encouragement and support through the process. That academic work would provide the very foundations for this book.

I would also like thank my Newman University students who worked patiently with me in the development of the Promethean Measurement Tool – helping me to make this a more user friendly online tool and experience.

Finally, I would like to thank my two brother in laws Clyde Corkhill and Bradley Hart. It was observing them as they navigated the challenges of mid and late career job loss that initially inspired my research journey. Seeing this treacherous landscape through their experiences gave me an appreciation of the risks, trials and incredibly high stakes of such undertakings.

PREFACE

A few years ago, my wife and I settled in for a holiday evening with our two college-age children. As with many families, it is our tradition to play board or card games to pass an evening at home over the Christmas holidays. When we discussed possible games to play, one of our kids suggested "Presidents and Paupers."

Our son explained it was a game of strategy that awarded advantages to the leaders (presidents) and disadvantages to the laggards (paupers). At the beginning of each hand, my son noted, the winner of the previous round would receive the two best cards from the person in fourth position, and the person in second position would receive the best card from the person in third position. The first and second players would then give their worst two and one cards, respectively, to the other two players. In this way, the paupers—the players in the third and fourth positions—would have disadvantages during the next round of play.

As the game began, my wife and I swiftly began to lose. As such, we had to deal with the disadvantages the rules of the game dealt us. After every hand we lost, my wife and I had to surrender our best cards to our kids. As the night proceeded, the punitive nature of the game increasingly presented itself, as our children continued to win and my wife and I continued to lose.

Although we were losing, we both continued play and enjoyed the frivolity of the evening. We were happy to be home with family rather than dealing with the stresses of business and other real-world problems. We convinced ourselves that our poor performance in the game was not because we were not skilled at strategy or cards in general; it was simply a matter of luck. Therefore, the fact that we were losing did not matter, and we focused more on the opportunity to enjoy our time with the family.

But despite this introspective pep talk, as the evening progressed and my wife and I continued to lose, I was surprised to feel uneasy emotions bubble up. I felt bewildered by the challenge of trying to overcome the structural constraints of the game. It seemed there was no way for myself and my wife to win, or even break even, much less change our overall fortunes within the contest.

Why was this bothering me so much? After all, it was just a silly game. Because of the rules of the contest, it was evident that the deck was definitively stacked against us. But as I thought about why this innocent game bothered me so much, I began to see and recognize the parallels between our current business realities and that of the game's structure and rules. Upon much reflection, it became increasingly obvious to me that the game's rules were similarly imbalanced to the rules of the game in the industry we conducted business and competed in.

Although I had recently completed research and my doctoral dissertation on the topic of change and convulsive environments, this seemingly innocuous evening would further enlighten me on a topic that is rapidly growing in pervasiveness in our social and economic landscape.

STRUCTURAL INEQUITIES AND IMBALANCE

There is much discussion currently about structural inequities and imbalances, particularly in our economic, social, and cultural landscapes. Much of the dialogue centers on race, gender, and historically unfair (even corrupt) societal as well as governmental practices and systems. While most will acknowledge that such unfairness and even exploitation has and currently still exists, we are struggling mightily in regard to the essential pathways, funding mechanisms, and appropriate time frames to fix such imbalances.

This point being acknowledged, the fact remains that in capitalistic systems, such inequities and disparities are in fact baked in, and are even appropriate and desired. Businesses and organizations worldwide work diligently to identify opportunities to tip the scales in their organization's favor via such devices as rules, regulations, and legislation, while at the same time stacking the deck against competitor businesses and organizations.

While it can seem brutal and unfair at times, it is part of the system as we know it and what we have traditionally and historically embraced. We make laws, prosecute offenders, and do our best to police systems and structures so that they are as fair as possible. But in the end, especially in recent times, it can seem there is little equity to be found.

Our recent pandemic and the resultant realities are just the latest glaring example of how wrong and imbalanced both world and economic structures can be toward selected (and less powerful) participants. While many well-positioned and politically influential multinational corporations are seemingly raking in record sales and profits via the pandemic, other economic participants are inversely expected to suspend business operations, lose employment, and bear the brunt of keeping national and global health environments safe and secure—all while receiving irregular and inconsequential remunerations for their efforts and sacrifice.

INTRODUCTION

Employment Placement Professional: Well … it was extremely stressful and intense [the period from 2008 through 2011]. As an outplacement contracting company, we worked with certain large employers in the region. We were getting flooded with people from the companies we were contracted with, there were many downsizings and in several instances … large-scale layoffs.

You know—it never ceases to amaze me with these mass layoffs … a person is one of two hundred people laid off over a period of a few days … they know it is a mass layoff event … You just can't believe how personally many of them take it—asking the same questions: Why me? What could I have done differently? Why wasn't I good enough?

Well, at least I never lost anyone through that period … I've had colleagues [in this profession] that did.

Straub/Researcher: Can you clarify what you mean by *lost someone*?

Employment Placement Professional: To suicide. [No expression; complete silence.] So … I am very thankful for that.

Straub/Researcher: [Continued silence].

Employment Placement Professional: Can I share something with you?

Straub/Researcher: Absolutely.

Employment Placement Professional: This has been very therapeutic … I don't talk to anyone about this stuff, not my husband, nobody in my family … It can be so disheartening, so sad. I just can't bring myself to do it …

As the researcher conducting this particular interview in 2012 during the qualitative portion of my doctoral research journey, I can tell you I will never forget this interchange and experience. During the thirty seconds of silence that followed the word *suicide*, I waited for the follow-up statement, a look of reassurance, or at least an acknowledgement of the intensity of what had just happened—what had been said. It did not take place; just silence and a deadpan, almost unemotional look on the interviewee's face that told another story in itself—that this was somehow normal, just the landscape such individuals traversed regularly in the course of their professional lives.

Before each of the chapters in this book, I will share a similar real-world example from my research—samples of some of the most impactful and interesting interviews I did in my investigative journey. Many have a happy ending; some do not. That is in essence the nature of the topic at hand.

As we begin our journey together, I would note that it is with trepidation that I write this book. To be the harbinger of future events, especially ones that are likely not pleasant to consider, is a somewhat onerous task. That being said, I feel it is vitally important to offer this analysis, critique, and possible framework for moving through some of the increasingly challenging times that may present themselves in the coming decades.

There might be a legitimate debate as to whether this manuscript and a new framework is needed at all. A few years ago, while I was presenting my findings and the foundations of this book, an academic colleague questioned the need for it. He observed, somewhat legitimately, that economies, societies, and cultures are very resilient and have taken such hits as the Great Depression, 9/11, and 2008 yet remained standing, eventually recovering with little noticeable long-term impact.

While there is a case to be made for his position, I pointed out that my associate, while technically correct, was missing a very key and very real dimension. While he might have a solid point on the bigger or macro environment, what he was missing, and failing to adequately consider, was the impact on select individuals, industries, and even entire regions.

Many times, subsets of individuals and segments of economies do not recover entirely or even at all. Post-Depression and post-2008, there were many individuals and regions that never fully recovered. After the COVID-19 pandemic, there will be huge swaths of business and personal bankruptcies. Though we may collectively hit the reset button and attempt to move on from this period, many will never fully recover.

CONVULSIONS AND WHY THEY ARE IMPORTANT

While I could not locate a specific definition for *economic convulsion*, a generally utilized definition of recession points to two consecutive quarters of negative real growth in gross domestic product. Therefore, it was necessary to utilize the broad definition of the word *convulsion*, which I feel is acceptable, even appropriate for the purpose of this work: "an abnormal violent and involuntary contraction or series of contractions … seizure … a violent disturbance … an uncontrollable fit."[1] While the definition is technically a portrayal of what happens with regard to human physiology, it seems to me that these same descriptors can be appropriately utilized when describing convulsions in our economic as well as social and cultural environments.

To supplement this assertion, we can also highlight the synonyms for the word convulsion: "bouleversement, cataclysm, earthquake, paroxysm, storm, tempest, tumult, upheaval, uproar." As a point of further explanation, when we discuss convulsions within this work, we are talking about huge-scale, disruptive, and catastrophic events. These could come in the form of weather events, natural disasters, pandemics, political instability, technological miscalculation, or social/cultural movements. Examples from the past couple of centuries would include wars (the Civil War and world wars), the Great Depression, the 2008 global economic collapse, and finally the COVID-19 pandemic.

I hope this provides a better understanding of what defines and constitutes convulsive events. In short, these are the events that define our lives and even generational landscapes.

With this manuscript, it is not my intent to cast judgment (or guilt) on particular generations, groups, or segments of our

---

1 *Merriam-Webster's Collegiate Dictionary*, s.v. "convulsion," accessed August 25, 2021, https://unabridged.merriam-webster.com/collegiate/convulsion.

society or economy. What has and will take place economically, socially, and culturally was in many ways almost destined to happen for a multitude of reasons. While there are many ways this case could be made, I will highlight what I refer to as the *quadfecta* of events that created a perfect storm: globalism, the widespread use of debt and leverage, the exponential growth of technological innovation, and the imperfect governmental structures and systems utilized in the United States and other regions of the world. While all four of these substantive progressions have been increasing and impacting populations for hundreds of years, their importance has grown significantly in the past five decades to create economic and societal complexities like never before.

GLOBALISM

As we discuss migratory histories and patterns early in the book, we will also discuss the history of globalism and its potential future progressions. However, it is imperative to acknowledge that the move to globalism is intricately tied to technological innovation, particularly the growth of communication and more sophisticated modes of transportation and travel. Before the advent of modern mass transportation, populations were constrained to more regional (even tribal) societal and economic systems, with people living their entire lives in relatively small parts of their country of origin or region of the world.

Particularly with the advent of air travel, individuals can seamlessly (and relatively inexpensively) circle the globe in a matter of days. These prospects introduce us to new cultures with corresponding opportunities, threats, and challenges, most recently evidenced by unprecedented global economic growth as well as the onslaught of the coronavirus pandemic.

WIDESPREAD UTILIZATION OF DEBT AND LEVERAGE

While debt and credit are wonderful tools that have provided for much growth, prosperity, and advancement, their enormous potential comes with very real negatives. The utilization and democratization of widespread debt and credit is a fairly recent phenomenon, and we are struggling as individuals, cities, states, and nations with the proper usage of such tools.

The growth of such instruments has been widely encouraged by financial and economic leaders and even heads of state, who cheer enthusiastically while creating economic policies and structures to perpetuate such usage and practices. The near zero percent interest and easy-money policies handed down from entities such as the US Federal Reserve have particularly encouraged and even necessitated such practices.

EXPONENTIAL GROWTH OF TECHNOLOGICAL INNOVATION

Technological innovation has been with us for centuries (arguably thousands of years) and will continue as we progress. What is noteworthy in recent decades is the pace of change in the current landscape, particularly the advent of the internet, smartphones, travel, and lately artificial intelligence.

We will highlight the many ways this has impacted our societies and cultures as well as economic and governmental structures. We will also show the ways in which we struggle to catch up and adapt to such momentous progressions.

FLAWED GOVERNMENTAL STRUCTURES AND SYSTEMS

A primary challenge of governmental systems is that much like technology, they are obsolete almost the moment they are conceptualized and designed. This is especially true when you assess current-day governmental structures, most designed hundreds of years ago and only occasionally updated or tweaked in meaningful ways. These systems were designed well before the industrial and technological revolutions and globalization, as well as advances in communication and travel. This leaves the government struggling mightily to monitor and manage systems and activities that seem way beyond the designers' reach, understanding, capability, and even initial intention.

With this as our backdrop and landscape, is it any wonder that our society, culture, economy, and political system—and the antiquated frameworks supporting them—have become exceedingly strained? While utilizing systems and frameworks that are many times decades if not centuries old, we struggle to stay ahead of tsunami-like movements and convulsions in our macro environment. The models and frameworks that have worked in the past will likely not work as successfully, if at all, moving forward. Many indicators point to these socioeconomic movements as being permanent shifts. New paradigms and tools will be needed as a result.

THE MISSION OF THIS BOOK

This book will attempt to envision what the path forward might look like, as well as the models, structures, and frameworks to support such passageways. We will focus on the micro rather than the macro, helping to manage and improve the plight of individuals as well as the smaller subsets within our economies and environments—those groupings that are often forgotten and even left behind during dramatic and fast-moving socioeconomic shifts.

PREVIEW AND STRUCTURE OF THE BOOK

In the course of this book, I will introduce you to the model of 6e Thinking. This proposed model will serve as a different way to think about our lives and practices in the face of the important changes and evolutions I have just highlighted. However, before I introduce you to this framework as well as the research and structure that produced it, I would like to highlight the layout and organization of the book itself.

THE STORY OF MY FAMILY AND OUR COMPANY

This will be intentionally brief and will occur in six parts, with a small story at the beginning of each part of the book. It is my feeling that what my family and business has gone through serves as a good case study and microcosm for what I will be highlighting and discussing throughout the book. It is with this intent that I share our story and experience.

Within this story, I will reveal the different aspects and components of 6e Thinking that were at play and deployed within the emphasized events. I will also show the realities, complexities, and challenges that presented themselves along with each aspect and scenario.

While much of the story of my family and our company is successful and uplifting, you will see that we faced definite challenges, some of which would eventually force difficult decisions and result in the sale of the family business. While it was by most measures a successful sale and exit from the industry, you will see that it came with some pain, dissension, and even controversy within the family and organization.

The sharing of these experiences will hopefully demonstrate the very real challenges that individuals and organizations can face as they proceed down such uncertain passageways.

PARTS ONE THROUGH FOUR

I have kept this book relatively constrained by design. My goal was to have a book that would be easy to read and comprehend as well as fewer than two hundred pages in length. My goal was for this book to seem somewhat conversational in its approach.

There are four parts to the book, each designed to take the reader through the history that brought us to this point… provide an acknowledgement about where we are and how we got here; and finally explain what we can do to manage in such demanding environments. I pay particular attention to the historical context-the growth, the advancement and even the cultural division.

I will also introduce you to the research and emergent framework that this work is based on. It is in large part the result of my 2010 to 2014 research completed as part of the dissertation requirements for my doctoral journey while at Case Western Reserve University. The Promethean Framework that emerged from this educational journey is highlighted and shown to eventually transform into the central model of this book and the concept of 6e Thinking.

THE PROMETHEAN FRAMEWORK MEASUREMENT INSTRUMENT

At the end of the book (Appendix C), I am including the link to take the actual survey that served to gather data for the resultant Promethean Framework and Theory. This survey can be taken online, and the results will be automatically scored and recorded so that they can be added to our bed of data and analyzed for future studies on the topic of managing lives and careers in convulsive environments.

WELCOME TO 6E THINKING

At this time, I want to introduce you to the model of 6e Thinking. This will serve as a framework as we move forward, and these models and practices will be highlighted and demonstrated in the stories I share regarding my personal as well as business journey and experiences. The tenets of 6e Thinking are as follows:

- adaptability and toughness
- practicality
- strong and stable relationships
- financial stewardship
- positivity
- scenario planning
- physical and mental vitality
- lifelong learning
- life and career transformation

WHAT I HOPE TO ACCOMPLISH

First, I want to identify historical and recent phenomenon and examine how they helped contribute to our current dysfunctional and complicated societal, cultural, and economic environment and circumstances. Second, I would like to provide careerists enough lead time to acclimate and adapt to such realities. Third, I hope to highlight a framework and provide a road map for surviving, even prospering, in the challenging environments to come. Finally, I will suggest possible fixes or resets to macro systems and processes that are damaged and taking us, repeatedly, down such untenable pathways.

I hope you enjoy this book and find it of value.

THE FIRST CONVULSION:
THE FAMILY BUSINESS

COMPONENTS OF 6E THINKING

- scenario planning
- adaptability and toughness
- lifelong learning

Before each part of this book, I will highlight examples of convulsive events from my own personal and business experience. Additionally, I will point to the aspects of 6e Thinking (and practices) that made the biggest impact on my family's success in pushing through these disruptive periods in our shared personal and business experiences.

My family's story is born in a way from the ashes of a previous and major convulsive event: the loss of my father's first career. My father, Walter J. Straub, who was always referred to as Wally, was an incredibly intelligent individual and businessman. His journey started on a farm in Central Kansas in the first half of the twentieth century. Born into hardship, his earliest years were marked by both the Great Depression and the associated period known as the Dirty Thirties. As evidence of his early dust-bowl years, he bore scars of a procedure performed when he was a child, with a physician inserting a tube into his lung to facilitate breathing and sufficient oxygen levels, saving his young life.

Wally grew up in a large family, working on the farm evenings and weekends while also juggling the demands of school. That is, until his junior year in high school when his father told him to drop out so he could devote the majority of his time to the family farming operation. While Wally was devastated at this prospect, he did as he was told because of the needs of the family and the fact that his older brothers were both serving in the waning stages of the Second World War. As was his tendency, Wally looked at the negative as an opportunity to learn to work hard and help the family, as well as find different pathways to acquire the knowledge and skills he knew would help him attain his future ambitions.

Early in his career, Wally would go to work for one of the largest International Harvester truck dealerships in North America: Gibson Titus and Stafford (GT&S). He would learn the trade of diesel mechanic and, within a decade, become one of the most accomplished and respected mechanics in the Midwest. I remember those days fondly, traipsing around that dealership with abandon. Every now and then, Mr. Titus would gingerly scold me, but many times he would give me a small toy truck to play with while my dad worked with customers.

The peak period for the business was in the 1960s and early '70s. The farming and trucking industries kept the GT&S dealership humming, running three shifts, 24/7, 365 days a year. Then came the mid- to late 1970s, when the trucking industry began to wane due to high interest rates and rising fuel prices. Within a decade, the company's fortunes would diminish dramatically and never recover. By this time, my father was a top salesman in the truck division and helped manage the overall dealership operation as well. Knowing the risks of a volatile industry, he had taken the truck sales position as an opportunity to learn new skills and grow his contacts within the business and commercial landscape.

With the growing uncertainty of his situation, Wally decided to take an outsized risk. In 1971, he and my brother Ron bought a 50 percent stake in an oil service company. My brother was in his early college years, and my parents had some money set aside for his educational endeavors.

Ron, who also had ambitions of being an entrepreneur, offered to contribute his college savings as part of the seed capital to purchase the 50 percent stake in this fledgling company. Wally was impressed and appreciative, and with that, the two began what would be a nearly fifty-year journey with the birth of the Straub Companies.

What seemed like a great opportunity was indeed initially a very profitable endeavor. However, due to the Arab oil embargo and the irregular conditions that followed, these lucrative times would be cut short. By the early 1980s, oil prices had plummeted, and the once prosperous industry was reeling on all fronts.

This period would present the young company with some of its most significant challenges—but it would also provide one of the major opportunities of the firm's early history.

PART ONE

THE FIVE EVOLUTIONS

Evolution: The gradual development of something, especially from a simple to a more complex form.—**Oxford Dictionary**

Those who do not move, do not notice their chains.—**Rosa Luxemburg**

It is not the strongest or the most intelligent who will survive but those who can best manage change.—**Leon C. Megginson**

In the above definition of the word *evolution*, it would be pertinent to note the word *gradual*. Through human history, mankind has made strides and steady progress incrementally, with change and most advances being marked in decades, even centuries. The challenge facing us currently is that the pace of change has escalated significantly in the past hundred years and has been even more profound in the past twenty to fifty years. This escalation of the pace of change and how we keep in step with it will be much of the focus of this work. How we and future generations deal with these dramatic and challenging environments will no doubt be the subject of history books well into the future.

While there are legitimate arguments and debates in regard to what would be considered the most significant evolutions in human history, for the purposes of this work, we will consider five that have been predominant in the development of modern-day humankind. Two of these evolutions have to do with the flow of peoples and resources, two with technology and industrialization, and the last relates to the mounting social, cultural, and political divisions. The five evolutions that will be highlighted are as follows:

1. Mobility and migration
2. Industrialization
3. Globalization
4. The Explosion of Technological and Financial Sophistication
5. The Great Divide and the Post-Truth World

Correspondingly, through the course of our examination, we will explore the significant realities, opportunities, and challenges of each evolutionary movement.

The significance in visiting these five evolutions of civilization is so that we can examine valuable lessons learned as well as opportunities presented, so that these might serve as a road map for the many trials we will face moving forward. While it is obvious that many of the issues we face are new and unique, there are also many historical similarities, such as industrialization, technological growth, and globalization. All of these have been emerging over many centuries, posing distinct challenges and opportunities at every turn.

It is also important to acknowledge that evolution and change are not only a constant but also a desired state. If living beings and societies don't evolve and change, they risk their own demise. While it is appropriate to highlight that through the centuries economies, countries, and global regions have successfully adapted (in most cases) to large and significant changes and evolutions, the same reality is not the case for individuals, sectors of economies, and smaller regions and cities.

It is my hope that fully examining these five evolutions will illustrate the futility of believing that we will stop or even deter current and future trends. In the context of history, it becomes painfully evident that the best we can do is slow the tide a bit (via regulation, legislation, cultural and societal pressure, etc.), never fully stopping its movement and progress.

1
THE FIRST EVOLUTION: MOBILITY AND MIGRATION

Research Participant: I had the job for twenty-five years. It was not totally unexpected when I lost it; the company had financial problems for the past ten years. But having been there for so many years and being fifty years of age … it was still devastating and concerning.

I had done quite a bit of research. From what I was seeing, getting reemployed past the age of fifty is much more difficult. It seemed the first six to nine months was going to be very crucial.

What I was seeing made me think that if I got past one year unemployed, I could be flirting with un-employability. It was scary to think …

Straub/Researcher: How did your search go?

Research Participant: It was a very slow go. You can never prove it (or even think it is worth it to fight) but you feel your age is working against you somewhat.

Straub/Researcher: Were you successful in getting reemployed?

Research Participant: Yes ... but it was not a straight line. There were detours involved.

Straub/Researcher: Could you describe what you are referring to?

Research Participant: My search was not going well. I was about seven months into it and was having very little luck. One of my goals was to stay in the area. We had a beautiful home, and our life was here.

About that time, the BP pipeline incident happened down south, and I was able to kind of pause the clock a bit by working down there.

Straub/Researcher: Can you describe what you mean by *pausing the clock*?

Research Participant: Yes. I worked down there for about four months. They would fly me in and out. I would work for a month and then come home for a month.

As I said—I felt it kind of paused the one-year time clock. I was still able to work on my job search over the internet. Then I was able to do interviews when I got home. It actually worked pretty well. The folks that I interviewed with seemed really impressed that I was willing to go the extra mile to work. I had some great stories to tell.

Straub/Researcher: You got reemployed?

Research Participant: I did, after about one year ... ended up getting a better job with a more stable company. I did end up taking about a 15 percent pay cut, but I was glad to have a full-time job with benefits. I felt that eventually I would get back to where I was again.

Straub/Researcher: Did that actually happen?

Research Participant: It did. It took me about two years to get back to where I was. By the fourth year, I was about 10 percent above where I was in my previous job ... I feel my prospects and earning potential are very good going forward.

Straub/Researcher: What did you ultimately take away from this experience?

Research Participant: That you have to take care of the long term and the big picture. Sure, I took a pay cut, but I didn't have to move. My wife had a good job ... we were able to keep our life intact. It was definitely worth it.

Straub/Researcher: Anything else you would like to add or highlight?

Research Participant: Yes ... just the importance of and the value of networks.

Human Migration: The movement by people from one place to another, particularly different countries, with the intention of settling temporarily or permanently in the new location. It typically involves movements over long distances and from one country or region to another.—***Wikipedia***

A couple of the challenges as we attempt to wrap our (metaphorical) arms around the subject of mobility and migration are a definition of terms as well as the intense passion that currently surrounds the topic. We will not only work with the definition of terms but also the application of such language.

There are three primary terms we will work with through the course of our discussion: mobility, migration, and immigration. Mobility is simple enough, so we will begin there. In its purest and most condensed form, *mobility* is defined as "the ability to move freely and be easily moved."[2] This can be a practical and foundational element of Western democracies, in terms of not only physical movements but also cultural, political, and economic movements. Most would agree this is an inherent desire of peoples across the world.

Next, we will explore the differing definitions in regard to *migration* and *immigration*. Part of the problem in discussing such issues rationally and fairly is that we misidentify and even conflate the terms. The basic definition of migration deals with "the process of animals travelling to a different place, usually when the season changes."[3] A further human and economic meaning deals with "the process of a person or people travelling to a new place or country, usually in order to find work and live there temporarily or permanently."[4]

Immigration, on the other hand, describes "the process of

---

2 Cambridge Dictionary, s.v. "mobility," accessed May 6, 2021, https://dictionary.cambridge.org/us/dictionary/english/mobility.

3 Cambridge Dictionary, s.v. "migration," accessed May 6, 2021, https://dictionary.cambridge.org/us/dictionary/english/migration.

4 Cambridge Dictionary, s.v. "migration," accessed May 6, 2021, https://dictionary.cambridge.org/us/dictionary/english/migration.

coming to a country in order to live in it permanently."[5] This permanence is behind much of the intensity and complexity associated with the issue and results in considerable controversy in many regions of the world.

Before we dive into the issues, controversies, and complications of the subjects at hand, let's first look at the history, both ancient and modern, of migration and immigration patterns. In doing so, we will find that the problems, patterns, and cultural issues we are contending with and experiencing currently are not new; they are, in many ways, as old as human history itself.[6] Such disputes result from the desire and ambition of large segments of populations to search for opportunity, safety, and a better life for themselves and their families.

Why do people migrate? Are the reasons significantly different than in past centuries? While there are (and have been) a myriad of reasons for migration, the normal, even predictable ones still exist and have been constant. There are four major influences on and types of migration: invasion or conquest, poor wages or lack of jobs, famine or natural disaster, and family separation.[7] It is important to note that nomadic movements are not normally thought of or considered *migration*, as they are usually seasonal or temporary movements with no intent to settle permanently in the new place or location.

---

5 Cambridge Dictionary, s.v. "immigration," accessed May 6, 2021, https://dictionary.cambridge.org/us/dictionary/english/immigration.

6 History.com, "U.S. Immigration Timeline," https://www.history.com/topics/immigration/immigration-united-states-timeline, last modified May 14, 2019.

7 R. Woldeab, "Why Do People Migrate? The 4 Most Common Types of Migration," *Population Education* (October 30, 2019), https://populationeducation.org/why-do-people-migrate-the-4-most-common-types-of-migration/.

Migration typically takes shape in a few different and often dramatic ways. Much of historical and even current-day migration takes place due to military conflicts that result in the flight of refugees because of fear of expulsion and, in the worst cases, the threat of forced enslavement or even physical harm.[8] The best-case scenario for many migrants is to search out economic, religious, and political opportunity elsewhere.

Migration has traditionally been viewed, at a macro level, as a symbol of profound human ambition and development. It has been further viewed and even celebrated as a natural social phenomenon. However, at a micro level, it is currently and consistently viewed by differing elements as a political and economic annoyance, even a threat.

As of 2019, about 3.5 percent of the world's population live away from their place of birth/origin.[9] Most would agree this is a relatively minor portion of the global population; however, this small percentage has outsized implications and controversies and can result in immense problems in many regions of the world.

THE HISTORY OF GLOBAL MIGRATION (ANCIENT)

There are two types of and reasons for migration, called *push and pull factors*. Push factors result in emigration; some of the reasons for this type of movement include poverty, war, and environmental disasters. Pull factors result in immigration for

---

8 Wikipedia, s.v. "Human Migration," last modified August 14, 2021, https://en.wikipedia.org/wiki/Human_migration.

9 California Academy of Sciences, "Interactive Human Migration Map," 2016.

such reasons as economic opportunity as well as political and/ or religious freedom.

The following key dates of ancient migration help put into perspective current-day problems and complexities, further illustrating the impact of such patterns on human history:

- **70,000 years ago**, irregular weather patterns caused the first known migrations from East Africa to the farther reaches of the continent.
- **60,000 years ago**, the first humans left Africa for India and eventually reached Australia 50,000 years ago. Around the same period, a second group crossed the Red Sea, eventually populating the Middle East and Central Asia.
- **40,000 years ago**, humans entered Europe through the southeastern regions of the globe. Neanderthals went extinct shortly thereafter.
- **25,000 years ago**, Earth entered the last vestiges of the Ice Age.
- **15,000 years ago**, the first humans crossed the Bering Strait into the Americas.
- **12,000 years ago**, the agricultural revolution began. [10]

It would seem when viewing such significant stages of migration through the entirety of human history that we have as much chance of substantially influencing these patterns as changing the shape and nature of the continents themselves.

---

[10] California Academy of Sciences, "Interactive Human Migration Map," 2016.

GLOBAL MIGRATION PATTERNS (CONTEMPORARY)

Significant amounts of migration taking place currently are voluntary, as careerists and individuals seek out opportunity and adventure in faraway countries and regions. Most are not running *from* anything but *toward* a more interesting and enticing future. With that being said, many of the same dark reasons that people migrated before are still present, such as war, discrimination, political unrest, and poverty.

Health pandemics have been a reality and a threat throughout human history. However, the peril has never seemed more real and had such a global impact as that of the current COVID-19 contagion. How will this affect migratory patterns in coming decades? Interestingly, there seem few places to escape the challenges associated with these medical realities and challenges.

FUTURE AND PREDICTED MIGRATION PATTERNS

While there is no doubt that future migration patterns will be different (even evolved), they will likely be hindered and stifled by the stir of nationalism and populist political uprisings. This being said, there is little doubt that such movements will be denied. Despite our current pandemic and other significant challenges, there are simply too many drivers and opportunities associated with globalism. It seems unlikely we will ever get that figurative genie back in the bottle. Businesses and their proxies will continue to force the march of globalism, chasing after profits and opportunities too lucrative to be denied.[11] The

---

[11] S. Donnan, and L. Leatherby, "Globalization Isn't Dying, It's Just Evolving," *Bloomberg* (July 23, 2019).

free movement of skilled (and cheap) labor and opportunities across borders will continue to be the goal of corporate and moneyed interests.

There will no doubt be many more convulsive events associated with globalism, including political unrest, dramatic cultural shifts, and climate instabilities that dislodge and dislocate vast swaths of people and regional populations. National governments will need to get innovative and identify better, more permanent, and more compassionate ways of dealing with these irregular waves of global nomads.

MIGRATION CONTROVERSIES

Much of the debate concerning migration and immigration centers on nation-state sovereignty and the perceptions and realities of legal and illegal immigration. Further complicating the matter is that the topic is so inflammatory, even toxic, that few politicians see any upside to dealing with it effectively, sustainably, and for the benefit of the majority of stakeholders.

A substantial point of contention is the consideration of what immigration, both legal and illegal, costs specific realms of society and the economy.[12] There are some desirable immigrants for all countries, such as those who possess wanted skills and abilities; many of these have the option of almost unlimited stays and even preferential treatment for citizenship. The most controversial immigrants are those fleeing oppression in home countries and coming to contest and compete for lower and midrange jobs. Additionally, there is a perception and

12 C. Felter, D. Renwick, and A. Cheatham, "The U.S. Immigration Debate," *Council on Foreign Relations* 100 (June 23, 2020).

potential reality that the destination countries' lax immigration systems and social safety net programs can be an attraction and may be abused by migrant groups and populations.

A concern for many countries is that they can be overrun with immigrant populations who will then have sufficient numbers and power at the polls to take over entire regions utilizing legal democratic processes. These very scenarios are currently playing out in certain regions of the world and even some sections of the United States, as more immigrants become naturalized citizens.[13]

Despite the current controversies globally, the United States remains one of the most welcoming and diverse countries by far, with 48.2 million immigrants. Second is Russia with 11.6 million, and third is Saudi Arabia with 10.8 million.[14] The main countries of origin for immigrants coming to the United States are Mexico (11.9 million), India (11.4 million), Russia (11.1 million), and China (8.3 million).[15]

---

[13] Steven E. Schier, "From Melting Pot to Centrifuge: Immigrants and American Politics," Brookings.edu, December 2002, https://www.brookings.edu/articles/from-melting-pot-to-centrifuge-immigrants-and-american-politics/.

[14] G. Pison, "Which Countries Have the Most Immigrants?" *World Economic Forum* (March 13, 2019).

[15] S. Camarota and K. Zeigler, "Record 44.5 Million Immigrants in 2017," *Center for Immigration Studies* (September 15, 2018).

OPPORTUNITIES, CHALLENGES, AND LESSONS LEARNED

OPPORTUNITIES

Among the greatest opportunities we have are the chance to raise standards of living throughout the world; to expand the known boundaries of cultures, resources, and knowledge through collaboration and cooperation; and to bring a renaissance of diversity and opportunity to the far reaches of physical boundaries and those of the human experience.

CHALLENGES

The challenges are substantial—a listing full of controversy and complications. The shock of cultural change and transformation will be present; additionally, there will be an acceptance that there can and will be subdivisions of national populations at greater economic risk. Some of those populations experiencing the very real possibility of being left behind and not sharing in the added prosperity that comes as a result of globalist policies.

Globalization exposes countries to significant economic, societal, and even health threats. The 2008 economic near-collapse and the 2020 Covid pandemic present stark examples of the kind of outsized misfortunes that a more globalized environment can bring about. Fights and skirmishes between globalists and nationalists are brewing on almost every continent. Until more equal disbursements of gains is realized, it will be easy for nationalists to continue to sell the premise that globalism is bad for the masses and will continue to result in increasing levels of prosperity, wealth and income disparity.

As more money is allowed into the political arena at every turn, well-heeled capitalists will likely continue to use this influence to stack the deck increasingly in their favor, further alienating and disenfranchising large swaths of the population. This could and likely will result in even more unrest, rioting, and danger for democracies throughout the Western world.

LESSONS LEARNED

Despite these challenges and many others, we will not be able to force a return to the realities of the past. Globalism will not go away. Nation-states cannot and will never be able to seal borders and satisfy all the desperate demands put forth by their citizenry and electorates.

Our opportunity will be to challenge elected representatives to identify and implement long-term and sustainable solutions to these complicated and important issues. It will be necessary to develop reimagined configurations to facilitate the humane and mutual management of all human resources, both domestic and immigrant. These must allow for more defined and predictable visa policies that will make stable levels of migration and immigration possible, as well as agreements requiring more countries to participate through funding and the providing of resources for settlement of temporary refugee populations.

Migration and mobility will always be with us. Humanity refuses to be constrained. While it can be slowed at times, the movement of peoples and populations to opportunities around the world will always be part of our dynamic and evolving global landscape.

There are many entrenched political and social forces vigorously fighting long-term solutions. However, some indications bring hope that the tide may be turning. A new, younger, and more progressive generation is making its voice heard and insisting on new and more humane ways of dealing with migration and immigration. Such forces seem to have a good foothold and are well positioned to impact the political debate in the decades to come.

6 KEY TAKEAWAYS: MOBILITY AND MIGRATION

1. Mobility and migration have been a part of human history since the dawn of time.
2. There is no perceived political upside to dealing with these complicated issues currently.
3. There are actual perverse disincentives that prevent our political class from dealing constructively and productively with such issues.
4. National borders matter, and nation-states must identify appropriate laws and structures that allow for healthy levels of immigration while protecting sovereignty.
5. We must all contribute to the debate and pull away from the hyperbolic propaganda on both sides of the spectrum.
6. The issue of mobility and migration will not go away. There is no getting the genie back in the bottle.

2
THE SECOND EVOLUTION: INDUSTRIALIZATION

Straub/Researcher: You noted earlier that you had lost a job that you had for quite some time … can you tell me about that experience?

Research Participant: Yes … well, that was devastating.

It was about five years ago, and I can remember it like it was yesterday. It was a (somewhat) sizeable company-wide layoff, but I was one of the few in my department.

Totally unexpected … hit me like a ton of bricks.

Straub/Researcher: What was going through your mind? What did you feel at that time?

Research Participant: It seemed very unfair. I had been there almost twenty-five years, and I had good evaluations all the way through … always been very loyal to the company. There were many people "left standing" that had much less time with the company, much less experience. I know some of it had to do with my age … how much I made.

They gave me boxes and thirty minutes to pack up my personal effects. I was watched the entire time by a security official.

Straub/Researcher: Anything else you would like to share about the experience?

Research Participant: Just how incredibly heartbreaking and humiliating it was to be escorted out of the building by security … I had been with them over half of my life, and it was like they couldn't trust me to leave without stealing something or causing some type of commotion.

Intellectually, I got it. I had seen people mess up computers, cause a scene … all of the things they were worried about with me. But it still hurt … felt I should have been treated differently.

What hurt the most … these people I was walking by [on the way out of the building] were like a second family to me. I knew from much experience that the "work family" part was over also. This group, this family was gone just as sure as my job was … that was equally devastating to me.

When you walk out that door, it is somewhat like you contracted an infectious disease. Most of these people—you would not have much of a relationship with from this point on.

Straub/Researcher: Were you correct? Did you?

Research Participant: I was and I did not …

Straub/Researcher: You said it's been about five years … how long did it take you to recover from this experience?"

Research Participant: Give me your number … I will call you when it happens …

Researcher Note: *Approximately three years after this interview, this research participant called. She said that about a year after the interview, she had been successful in finding new employment—a good company and a good job. She was feeling much better about her situation and life in general. She had not forgotten our research interview and was impressed that I cared enough to give her my cell-phone number.*

Before we begin our journey through the industrialization of our nation and globe, I would like to start with an overview of the general trends and macro issues that lead to such transformations. There are several undeniable factors that have continually pushed mankind toward greater advancement and sophistication.

First is health and welfare. The oftentimes backbreaking work of manual labor historically has taken a toll on men, women, and children alike. While it provided steady work as well as relative income stability, it also came with little to no labor protections and oftentimes dismal, even abysmal, working conditions and environments.[16]

Second is ambition and the hope for a better life. As I alluded to in the previous chapter, there has constantly been an aspiration that individuals and families could move toward more stable, even middle-class lifestyles. Such a life and career would allow for stable work, increased leisure time, and higher levels of financial independence and security.

Finally, the general competitive business and economic environment constantly pushes leaders and their organizations to innovate and improve products and services. This drive and importance was once motivated solely by regional concerns; however, as travel and communication have increased, that concern has moved to the national and eventually the global realm.[17]

In this section of our investigation, we will look at the four industrial revolutions and highlight the impact these transformational periods had on individuals and work, as well as the general business environment and economies. We will also examine the causes of each as well as their time frames and evolutions.

THE FIRST INDUSTRIAL REVOLUTION

The first industrial revolution can best be characterized by the move to mechanization. It began in the last half of the eighteenth century and lasted through the early 1900s. This

[16] "Industrialization, Labor, and Life," *National Geographic* (January 27, 2020), https://www.nationalgeographic.org/article/industrialization-labor-and-life/12th-grade/.

[17] "Industrialization, Labor, and Life."

substantial move to mechanization was the primary reason jobs and production began the move toward cities and industrial centers and away from rural agricultural regions.[18]

This impactful period in economic history facilitated a global expansion in the period from 1760 to the early to mid-1800s. This period witnessed human and machinery production working side by side. Further, the invention of mechanized factory systems and structures dramatically boosted production and standards of living of workers, laying the initial foundations for the development of the middle class.

Much of the early growth and adoption of mechanization began in the world's leading economic centers, which were at that time centered in Great Britain and other European clusters. The foundations for this incredible period in our economic evolution were facilitated in the second half of the eighteenth century in the form of four key developments: textiles, steam power, iron production, and the invention of machine tools.

The textile industry was fueled by mechanized cotton spinning as well as the process of ginning cotton. Both were responsible for substantial gains in productivity of up to fifty times the previous rates of production. Additionally, steam power resulted in massive productivity increases while demonstrating a significant increase in efficiency in regard to fuel utilization.

Additional fuel and manufacturing efficiencies were facilitated by the use of coke (versus charcoal) in the production of iron. This utilization also facilitated much larger furnaces, resulting in greater economies of scale. Finally came the

---

[18] "Industrial Revolution Timeline," *History of Massachusetts Blog* (March 16, 2018), https://historyofmassachusetts.org/industrial-revolution-timeline/.

development of large-capacity tools, such as cutting lathes, milling, and cylinder boring machines. These technologies were in their infancy, but growth in these areas would have significant impact in the decades and centuries to follow.[19]

CAUSES

The causes of this period of human history are complicated and not entirely resolved. Much speculation centers on the fact that Britain possessed an abundance of natural resources during this period—including metal ores, coal, and hydro power—and a highly productive agricultural sector as well. Additional speculation points to the conclusion of the Black Death in the mid-fourteenth century, which put increasing pressure on production due to the decimation of that period's workforce. Finally, Britain's colonial structure resulted in the transfer of mechanization and technology to colonies across the globe, including America.[20]

As noted, there is debate over exact causes and timelines. It is possible the overriding pressure and demands were on providing better lives and opportunities to increasingly impatient populations. This push for and realization of better living standards would help governments keep the citizenry placated and relatively peaceable during this extended period.

---

[19] History.com, "Industrial Revolution," October 29, 2009, https://www.history.com/topics/industrial-revolution/industrial-revolution.

[20] Cynthia Stokes Brown, "The Industrial Revolution—Fossil Fuels, Steam Power, and the Rise of Manufacturing," Khan Academy, https://www.khanacademy.org/humanities/big-history-project/acceleration/bhp-acceleration/a/the-industrial-revolution.

IMPACTS ON WORKFORCE AND GENERAL ECONOMY

This period undoubtedly laid the foundation for the substantial individual and economic growth that would be experienced in the early to mid-twentieth century. Many aspects of life were positively and substantially impacted, including income, population, health, and standard of living. This period also developed the foundation for the middle-class lifestyles that would emerge, as well as the consumer class that would follow in the coming decades,[21] creating solid and sustainable demand for many products yet to come, such as automobiles, mechanized equipment, and housing, as well as the vibrant service economies to support them.

CONCLUSION

The benefits resulting from this period were substantial. The fruits of this time frame began to take mankind from a hand-to-mouth existence to one of relative prosperity and security. It would also pose challenges. This period would lead to a move from rural to more industrialized centers, challenging the bonds of family and community in a way never seen to this point.

Finally, the first industrial revolution would be a harbinger of future trends, creating and resulting in ever larger and increasingly powerful businesses. This newfound industrial financial power and influence would lead to severe abuses in the early 1900s and the advent of organized workforces

---

21 "Industrial Revolution Timeline," *History of Massachusetts Blog* (March 16, 2018), https://historyofmassachusetts.org/industrial-revolution-timeline/.

and eventually unionized labor movements to combat such imbalances.[22]

THE SECOND INDUSTRIAL REVOLUTION

Beginning in the latter half of the nineteenth century, we witness what is regularly referred to as the second industrial revolution. This period was brought about by massive technological advancements, primarily in the energy sector. Resulting from this dynamic era were the internal combustion engine, widespread steel usage and demand, chemical synthesis, and far-reaching methods of communication, such as the telegraph and telephone.

This second revolution grew to include chemicals and would eventually birth entire industries, predominant among them the petroleum sector, which would provide the energy for the advent and commercialization of automobiles and other motorized transportation. This creation of vehicles and air travel in the early part of the twentieth century would spur the move to more national and ultimately global markets.[23]

Eventually, large national and even global companies and industries would begin to emerge, resulting in the multinationals that currently dominate the global industrial landscape. With this growth in the general economy would come worker benefits, such as reduced work hours, safer working conditions, as well as stable and more secure incomes.

---

22 "Industrial Revolution Timeline," *History of Massachusetts Blog*, March 16, 2018, https://historyofmassachusetts.org/industrial-revolution-timeline/.

23 Ryan Englemen, "The Second Industrial Revolution, 1870–1914," U.S. History Scene, https://ushistoryscene.com/article/second-industrial-revolution/.

CAUSES

The roots of this dynamic period in human history were primarily the explosion of industrial advances and growth of key technologies. Chief among them were the combustion engine, petroleum, steel, and motorized transportation. Another chief driver was the invention of hydroelectric power and the electrification of industry and eventually much of the national landscape.

However, an equally important cause was perhaps the most under-credited: the growth in imagination and unbridled ambition in the United States, Europe, and certain other regions of the world.[24] These desires and ambitions grew and exploded just as surely as the technologies that provided the foundational elements for this dynamic and sustained period of growth.

IMPACTS ON WORKFORCE AND GENERAL ECONOMY

This period in history had a considerable impact on individuals, the workforce, and the general economy alike. Many of these were beneficial, such as increased standards of living, steadily growing economies, and the foundation of the middle classes that would follow. However, this period was not just filled with positives. Technological advancement would be utilized for darker forces as well, particularly in the area of warfare, eventually providing the foundational technologies and elements for the weapons of mass-destruction that would follow in the middle of the twentieth century.

---

[24] Englemen, "The Second Industrial Revolution, 1870–1914."

CONCLUSION

The second industrial revolution is considered by many to be the most dynamic in regard to its seemingly positive impact on and transformation of life, business, and even society. However, there are some who would argue that this dramatic period of transformation was not as constructive as it might have initially appeared. Many would point to the seeds of industrialized warfare planted during this period, as well as the beginning of the climate challenges that we currently face. While there is a wide range of opinions regarding this dynamic period and its impact, it cannot be disputed that it was in fact the precursor of the globalism and relative prosperity that we experience currently.[25]

THE THIRD INDUSTRIAL REVOLUTION

When the third industrial revolution begins is not widely agreed upon. Both the third and fourth revolutions are somewhat speculative at this point. If we are in actuality in the throes of the third industrial revolution, as many suspect, it likely began and took its place in the business and economic landscape in the last half of the twentieth century.[26] While the beginning of this period enjoys some consensus, there is not as much agreement in regard to its conclusion. Some would argue we are still in the

25 Englemen, "The Second Industrial Revolution, 1870–1914."

26 "The 4 Industrial Revolutions," *Institute of Entrepreneurship Development* (June 2019), https://ied.eu/project-updates/the-4-industrial-revolutions/#:~:text=The%20third%20revolution%20brought%20forth,expeditions%2C%20research%2C%20and%20biotechnology.

throes of the third revolution, while others contend the page has turned, and we are in the early phases of the fourth.

This revolution marks its beginnings with major, even revolutionary, advancements in power, communication, and technology. The reason it is believed these advancements were so transformational is that they ushered in a different stage of development. These progressions will be highlighted as we proceed to the next phase of our discussion.

Some of the major advancements during this period were impactful while simultaneously presenting substantial threats. Chief among these was nuclear power, which was further developed and advanced in the post-World War II era. Although the world had seen firsthand the incredible destruction this technology and weaponry could unleash, there was also no repudiating the unbelievable potential it held for the industrial and economic landscape.

Additionally, computerization and the invention of the microchip would advance large-scale information technology and the data sciences. These would lay the foundations for desktop computing and the data and information-management sectors that would eventually follow.

Finally, the landscape of travel and mass communication continued to expand and grow, to the point where globalization began to find its footing and would never look back, bringing the world together in terms of business and culture like never before.[27]

But as has been the case with each iteration of our progress, this period brought substantial challenges along with great

---

[27] Jeremy Rifkin, "Welcome to the Third Industrial Revolution," *Wharton Magazine* (Summer 2015), https://magazine.wharton.upenn.edu/issues/summer-2015/welcome-to-the-third-industrial-revolution/.

opportunities. These challenges were so considerable that they would ultimately threaten the very survival of populations in large expanses of the world.

CAUSES

We previously highlighted a major cause of the second revolution: the growth of imagination and ambition, particularly within Western civilizations and economies. In this third iteration, it was brought about by an uninhibited expansion of those same ambitions.

With an exponential growth of the middle class in many regions of the world, there was a demand and a desire for even more conveniences and even luxuries. As a post-World War II confidence bordering on arrogance continued to grow, the United States and some Western economies felt an optimism that there was little that they could not achieve and accomplish. These outsized desires were fueled by ever-larger machinery, seemingly unlimited sources of energy, sophisticated organizations, and economies of scale never experienced before.

Finally, the Cold War would soon result in ambitious arms, space, and political rivalries. Particularly as Russia and the United States emerged as the preeminent postwar superpowers, countries were forced to align and show loyalty to one or the other, dividing the world into a dangerous and counterproductive bipolarity not seen heretofore.[28]

---

[28] "The 4 Industrial Revolutions," *Institute of Entrepreneurship Development* (June 2019), https://ied.eu/project-updates/the-4-industrial-revolutions/#:~:text=The%20third%20revolution%20brought%20forth,expeditions%2C%20research%2C%20and%20biotechnology.

IMPACTS ON WORKFORCE AND GENERAL ECONOMY

Much of the impact of this third revolution on individuals and the economy was positive. In particular, in the Western world, incomes grew as there was continued mass migration from farms and small towns to the cities. As families increasingly had the means to travel and own automobiles, family sizes began to shrink, and the family unit and structure began to evolve and assume less important roles and significance.

Western economies continued to master and take advantage of the increased scale and opportunity that mechanized power and mass manufacturing provided. The US and Western economies would maintain their post-WWII dominance both politically and economically for the following four decades, eventually helping precipitate the collapse of its most substantial world rival, the USSR, in the process.[29]

This collapse would lead to a world with one preeminent power and allow the United States to consolidate its leadership position globally over the subsequent two-decade period. However, as is usually the case, this preeminence would not last long. Eventually, China and a reemerged Russia would grow to challenge the United States politically, militarily, and economically.[30] Additionally, many nefarious and increasingly sinister actors would emerge to challenge the very foundations of nation-states and democracies throughout the world.

---

[29] Sarah Pruitt, "The Post World War 2 Boom: How America Got Into Gear," *History: History Stories*, https://www.history.com/news/post-world-war-ii-boom-economy.

[30] Noam Chomsky, "American Decline: Causes and Consequences," Chomsky.info, https://chomsky.info/20110824/.

CONCLUSION

This period, while very productive and heady for the US and other Western countries, also laid the groundwork for a new and uncertain world order, as very real threats to the United States and Western democracies would emerge. As noted, not only a reborn Russia but also a more ambitious China would substantially challenge US and Western supremacy as never before.

Additionally, the advances in technology that led to incredible technological and mechanization gains would put the world in growing jeopardy via increasingly menacing weapons capabilities.[31] Conflicts in far-reaching parts of the world and the threat of nuclear war continued to be black clouds over much of the world in the last part of the twentieth century.

Not surprisingly, the unchallenged superiority of the US economic engine would not last indefinitely. Cheap labor and less-regulated manufacturing environments would eventually prove too tempting for the large and unwieldy global multinationals. Factory jobs would begin their mass exodus from the United States to foreign lands, beginning in the last half and continuing in earnest through the later stages of the twentieth century.

THE FOURTH INDUSTRIAL REVOLUTION

The fourth industrial revolution, as with the third, is currently more of a concept or idea. There is disagreement on the topic,

---

31 E. Steven Schoenherr, "The Digital Revolution," May 5, 2004, archived from the original on October 7, 2008.

with some thinking we are toward the end of the third while others feel we are at the beginning of the fourth. For the purposes of this work, we will assume and make a case for the latter.[32]

The reason it is plausible to make the case that we are in the early stages of the fourth revolution is due to the unique and defining characteristics of our current environment. There are four separate and defining features of our contemporary business and industrial realities that I will highlight. These serve as the foundation for why I feel the setting has changed and we have moved to a new, significant, and rapidly emerging landscape.

EXPONENTIAL INNOVATION

The exponential and convulsive change we are currently undergoing is unlike any period humankind has experienced before. This change is due in large part to globalism, as well as many and recent disruptive technologies—such as artificial intelligence, robotics, 3D printing, and nanotechnology—that are transforming life as we know it. Add to these accomplishments the medical advances associated with the mapping of the human genome, and it is quite possible we may not fully recognize our lives and careers in the coming decades.

---

[32] Klaus Schwab, "The Fourth Industrial Revolution—What It Means and How to Respond," *Foreign Affairs* (December 2015), https://www.foreignaffairs.com/articles/2015-12-12/fourth-industrial-revolution.

IMPACT ON CAREER PATHWAYS

The impact on lives and particularly careers from the aforementioned innovation will be both exciting and disconcerting. It is predicted there will be much more instability in jobs and careers. Currently, many struggle to make a living in the rapidly evolving gig economy, or as permanent adjuncts and part-time employees.[33]

As industries change and evolve, even the jobs that remain are at times changed so much they are unrecognizable. New models for transportation, services, and even manufacturing will have individuals at times working alongside their potential mechanized replacements, not knowing when and if they might be permanently replaced.

Globalism will continue to move forward. Despite temporary setbacks like the pandemic, the temptation of worldwide markets, cheap labor, and reduced regulation are simply too tempting for businesses to resist. It will likely continue to fuel the income and wealth gap between the top 1 percent and the remainder of workforces and economic structures.

Through this progression, blue collar, manual labor, unionized, and even some lower-level professional jobs will be endangered. Those of higher-level professionals and technical/knowledge workers will fortuitously take up the slack, growing in value, prevalence and importance.[34]

---

33 Laura J. Thalacker, "How the Gig Economy Is Changing the Working World," Lawyer-Monthly.com, October 2020, https://www.lawyer-monthly.com/2020/10/how-the-gig-economy-is-changing-the-working-world/.

34 Bernard Marr, "Why Everyone Must Get Ready for the 4th Revolution," *Forbes* (April 2016), https://www.forbes.com/sites/bernardmarr/2016/

IMPACTS ON WORKFORCE, GENERAL ECONOMY, AND SOCIETY

While it can be noted that economies and civilizations are resilient, that unfortunately is not as true of individual economic participants. The aggregate of our larger economies and society have shown themselves to be very pliable—the Great Depression, the World Wars, 9/11, and even the early-twenty-first-century global financial crises were resolved and eventually dispatched. The overriding challenge is that people and individual careerists are not as pliable as economic systems. They often are not able to adapt as well or as efficiently, with some never effectively making the turn or ever getting their lives and careers back on successful or sustainable pathways.

As intelligence, knowledge, and sophistication become the new currency, even gospel, there will likely be small but significant swaths of individuals left behind, forever changing the landscape of towns, cities, even entire regions. Those left in the wake of these perpetual cycles of disruption and dismemberment will be left to redefine the very concept of identity, family, and community.

GLOBALIZATION

With the recent events surrounding the COVID-19 pandemic, it cannot be denied that globalization is a dynamic that will continue to define our social and economic landscape as we

---

04/05/why-everyone-must-get-ready-for-4th-industrial-revolution/?sh=2e6f0d3a3f90.

move forward.[35] These incredible worldwide forces have the potential to unleash unimaginable opportunities and challenges.

How governments and cultures are able to manage these trials and opportunities will define much of the landscape in the coming decades. Unfortunately, it seems we are destined to work with old, unworkable models and mindsets. We are headed for counterproductive ideological battles on almost every front, most countries caught in a perpetual doom loop of our own making, feeling trapped between powerful and immovable forces on all sides.

Despite these facts, there is no denying these global forces and their impacts. We will have to work together to identify the most mutually beneficial and practical ways forward as global participants and partners.

OPPORTUNITIES, CHALLENGES, AND LESSONS LEARNED

OPPORTUNITIES

The opportunities of greater industrialization and innovation are obvious. We have made tremendous strides in all aspects of industry, science, technology, and medicine. With the current landscape of technological, medical, and scientific improvements, we can only imagine the advances that might present themselves in the coming decades and centuries. It is also logical to anticipate the staggering creation of wealth and productivity in our national and global economies.

[35] Raphael S. Cohen, "Why COVID-19 Will Not Stop Globalization (Commentary)," *The Rand Blog* (April 2020), https://www.rand.org/blog/2020/04/why-covid-19-will-not-stop-globalization.html.

CHALLENGES

As has been the case historically, there are many challenges that we have and will continue to face as we acclimate to these new realities—including physical climate, economic fairness, and regulation, as well as managing the national and global complexities of such growth. Our societies, cultures, and economies have a somewhat irregular record to date in regard to managing such intricacies well and productively.

LESSONS LEARNED

While it is understandable that we debate whether we are in the throes of the later stages of the third revolution or the early stages of the fourth, there is no doubt that there is no one revolution. There has been a series of definable and dynamic phases, and these will certainly not be the last.

There will be several iterations of what industry is, what it looks like, as well as its impact and contribution to cultures and societies. While we will continue to debate the terms and pace of industrial change, hopefully societies and markets can find ways to redefine, retool, and retrain as efficiently as possible, allowing most economic participants to keep pace and remain financially sustainable throughout.

6 KEY TAKEAWAYS: INDUSTRIALIZATION

1. Industrialization in one form or another is centuries old, and its advancement (like technology) is increasing exponentially.
2. As in the traditional course of human history, there is great potential for abuse of power and exploitation of poorly positioned and powerless populations.
3. The wonders of industrial innovation present incredible opportunities for mankind to improve lives and provide increased standards of living in North America and globally.
4. Continued regulation and oversight by governments will likely be necessary to impose constraints and encourage equity of opportunity.
5. The fourth industrial revolution puts us on the precipice of next-level movements and increased convulsiveness.
6. Global standards, ethics, and laws will need to be evolved and enforced consistently to provide safe, productive, and beneficial working conditions.

3

THE THIRD EVOLUTION: GLOBALIZATION

Research Participant: It was a mass layoff event. They were shutting most of the plant and operations down. Moving it all down south.

Straub/Researcher: Down south?

Research Participant: To somewhere in Mexico … It was a major cost-reduction move. They assured us it was no reflection on us or the quality of work … just about cost. Didn't notice that anyone was comforted by that proclamation … but that's what they told us.

Straub/Researcher: Was it immediate? Did they assist in helping you find other employment? Provide outplacement assistance or other resources?

Research Participant: Sort of … This is where it gets kind of weird. The ones terminated immediately were given outplacement and other assistance finding a job. However, about half of us were offered the opportunity to stay on and train our replacements.

It was so surreal … they presented it to us like it was the best news and gift they ever gave to anyone. When they called us together for a separate meeting, I almost thought they were going to offer us our jobs back … the atmosphere and mood of the team seemed so positive and upbeat.

After the meeting … it felt like … just another level of humiliation. It seemed so degrading.

Straub/Researcher: Did you do it?

Research Participant: Yes … I needed the money, and it gave me additional time to find another job.

They weren't totally the devil … they gave me outplacement assistance, a decent severance package (at the end of training my guy), and any time off I needed for interviews.

Straub/Researcher: Was your job search successful?

Research Participant: It was … not quite the money I was making. But it was in the same city, full time, stable and had good benefits.

Straub/Researcher: Anything else you would like to share?

Research Participant: It was such an emotional roller coaster, such highs and lows … really intense. It was so strange. I got really tight with the guy who I trained. Wonderful guy with an awesome family … we have a standing invite

for him and his family to come see us in the US.
How weird it that?

The traditional definition of globalization refers to economic interests that develop international influence and begin to operate on an intercontinental scale. However, much like many other terms, this one has been hijacked and politicized.[36] The contemporary meaning highlights the growing interdependence of the world's economies, cultures, and populations. These realities have taken on more nuanced and even paranoid connotations, encompassing and even representing the forces of wealthy elites with hidden and nefarious agendas.[37]

Despite this fact and notwithstanding pandemics, world conflicts, and other major events, globalization will continue as a major driver of growth, wealth, and instability in the coming decades. While competing ideological and political forces will slow its progression at times, as noted previously, the possibilities and enticements are simply too appealing, too compelling to be denied.

What are some factors that could slow growth and possibly impact globalization? Initially, and most imminently, would be additional health issues via large-scale outbreaks and even future pandemic threats. It is hard to deny that, in regard to global health threats, there is the distinct sensation that recent events moved us to an entirely new level of global dependence

---

36 Cambridge Dictionary, s.v. "globalization," accessed May 6, 2021, https://dictionary.cambridge.org/us/dictionary/english/globalization.

37 "What Is Globalization? And How the Global Economy Shaped the United States?" *Peterson Institute for International Economics* (October 2018), https://www.piie.com/microsites/globalization/what-is-globalization#:~:text=Globalization%20is%20the%20word%20used,investment%2C%20people%2C%20and%20information.

and hazard. This looming danger now seems very real and menacing. Even if that is not actually the reality, there are those who will take advantage of the fear and paranoia for their own potential gain. There will likely be long-lasting tension and fear that could lead to rational (and irrational) constraint of trade and migration.

Next will be general affluence and opportunities for global travel as more regions of the world grow their middle and upper classes. Despite the impact of recent events, it seems certain that there will still be incredible potential for growth of middle-class sectors across the globe. As this occurs, there will be increasing demand for trade, travel, education, and entertainment.

While global travel will continue, it will be changed and impacted for a number of years.[38] However, the continued desire for mobility will lead to further immigration and migration as people experience different regions of the world, drawn by enticements and amenities.

Technologies such as 3D printing, robotics, communication, and artificial intelligence will continue to knock down physical barriers between economies and countries. Governments and nation-states will increasingly fight to stay in front of trends and happenings throughout the world, but they may fight a losing battle, even finding themselves struggling to stay relevant and in the mix.

As racial distinctions and lineages become less defined in the coming century, it will become progressively more difficult for countries (and entrenched forces) to define and identify

---

[38] Harriet Baskas, "Most of the Changes in Travel Will Likely Continue Beyond Covid-19, Experts Say," NBC News, December 2020, https://www.nbcnews.com/business/travel/most-changes-travel-will-likely-continue-beyond-covid-19-experts-n1250777.

the enemy abroad—those who must be denied a place, access, or citizenship.[39] Ultimately, one of the key elements of many democracies can and will be exploited, allowing those who have legally immigrated to vote and even majorly influence the political structures of their adopted homelands.

World nongovernmental organizations (NGOs) and regional trade blocks will provide convenient and relatively stable platforms for continued global ascendency. Organizations such as the United Nations (UN), World Health Organization (WHO), and International Monetary Fund (IMF) will push to lead and even lessen the impact on individuals, economies, and cultures as these global movements evolve. Consortiums such as the European Union (EU) and others will continue to make immigration and migration a more seamless process, attempting to educate nations and their peoples on the benefits of global compacts as well as more malleable economies and borders.

Finally, two emergent opportunities will press countries to compete and even form consortiums: the race for advantage in the rapidly melting polar icecaps as well as intergalactic dominance. As we increasingly tax our planet and ecosystems, the allure of finding the next region or even planetary system to conquer or exploit increases. These quests will be the domain of national interests, the very rich, and the very daring. It currently seems to be in process and shows no signs of abating.[40]

---

[39] Carol Spaulding-Kruse, "The Whole World Will Be Brown: We Can Change What Race Means," *Des Moines Register* (June 2017), https://www.desmoinesregister.com/story/opinion/columnists/iowa-view/2017/06/12/whole-world-brown/386728001/.

[40] Richard Kemeny, "As Countries Battle for Control of North Pole, Science Is the Ultimate Winner," *Science Magazine* (June 2019),

HISTORY OF GLOBALIZATION

Early globalization began around 90,000 BC as early humans moved from the continent of Africa to mid-Asia, then into the southern regions of Europe and Western India. To identify and acknowledge this early movement of humanity is to understand and acknowledge that humankind has always had the will to explore unidentified regions and expand our documented world.

Throughout history, governments and their peoples have fought battles and even wars to fend off interlopers and invaders. But much like trying to fight back the forces of a raging river, success was fleeting and oftentimes unsustainable. Perspective is important when looking at immigration trends. When viewed in decades and centuries, the onslaught seems to be managed and controlled; however, when viewed in thousand-year increments, resistance to such movements and trends looks much more problematic.

After the World Wars, and particularly World War II, it became increasingly evident that international migration and global proceedings needed to be managed and more effectively directed. The emergence of world organizations (such as the UN, WHO, and IMF) was part of this movement to organize and better control world forces and coordinate the leading nations' efforts. While these efforts have been viewed as largely successful, recently elected populist leaders, cultural movements, perceived corruption, and world events have brought their values and missions increasingly into question.

Globalization is currently in an increasing state of flux

---

https://www.sciencemag.org/news/2019/06/countries-battle-control-north-pole-science-ultimate-winner.

and uncertainty. The tug of war between globalist and anti-globalist forces is very real and has heated up significantly in recent decades. The anti-globalist forces have historically been viewed as fringe groups, out of touch with reality. However, in the past decade, they have found powerful allies and a voice with populist world leaders in the United States and Europe.[41]

Which way these forces and movements go moving forward depends on a much larger battle, one not only of theory and politics but also of practicality between the forces and philosophies of nationalism and globalism.

NATIONALISM VS. GLOBALIZATION

Before we explore the topic of nationalism versus globalism, it is necessary to consider how both have been politically co-opted and even skewered in ideological deliberations. *Nationalism* in recent years has been designated as a generally negative and judgmental connotation for white nationalism and even racism, while *globalism* has taken on equally sinister designations and comparisons.[42] It is important to note, when using the terms for the purposes of our discussion, that I will be utilizing the literal definitions and terms. There is no political or ideological intent in this writing.

Historically, nationalistic forces have been preeminent and undeniable. However, due to extremely violent and dangerous

[41] Liam Stack, "Globalism: A Far-Right Conspiracy Theory Buoyed by Trump," *The New York Times* (November 2016), https://www.nytimes.com/2016/11/15/us/politics/globalism-right-trump.html.

[42] Anne Sraders, "What is Nationalism? Its History And What It Means in 2018," Thestreet.com, July 2018, https://www.thestreet.com/politics/what-is-nationalism-14642847.

regional and even world wars, it has become increasingly evident that a different model is warranted. Regional skirmishes and wars have been part of the landscape for centuries. The wars between the European superpowers in the 1500s through World Wars I and II made it evident that such events could dramatically impact the delicate global balance, peace, and increasingly large populations.

Particularly after the world wars of the twentieth century, it became evident that conflicts could quickly escalate, bringing in wider swaths of militaries and their peoples. As the weaponry of warfare grew much more sophisticated, deadly, and barbaric, many nations have demanded interventions and structures that might prevent future conflicts. Leading the new world order was the United States, which emerged post–World War II as the preeminent and unchallenged global power. Following the founding of the UN came the WHO and the IMF.[43] These NGOs were to serve as the foundation of the new global structure and act as a needed safety valve and potential check on world tensions.

Unfortunately, their structures and power would ultimately serve to undermine their own sustainability and credibility. Unchallenged, arrogant, well-financed, and corrupt structures would emerge and wield their clout to dominate world events. While this would seem within their initial design and charter, this power would also pit them against powerful nation-states (particularly the United States, China, and Russia) that fund much of their budgets and can substantially impact their positioning in the international landscape.

---

[43] Sarah Pruitt, "The Post World War 2 Boom: How America Got Into Gear," History: History Stories, https://www.history.com/news/post-world-war-ii-boom-economy.

In the latter half of the twentieth century and the first decades of the twenty-first, global economic growth would escalate, resulting in increasingly powerful global multinational enterprises. Some of these corporations would dominate the prospects of entire regional economies, in some cases overpowering populations and labor markets in their wake. These businesses and their owners grew global portfolios of companies, resulting in immense wealth and power, and leaving many to wonder if the benefits of globalization were going to a select few well-connected and powerful elitists.[44]

In their wake, anti-globalist movements would emerge and became more noticeable and increasingly vocal. For several decades, their presence and impact were viewed as a minor nuisance—until their fears and concerns were given voice in the early twenty-first century by American political populists like Donald Trump and Bernie Sanders.

With the ascension of such populist leaders to the highest levels of government in the United States and Europe, the anti-globalist forces had a voice, connections, and influence. This sentiment and passion led to movements like Occupy Wall Street and eventually Brexit and the election of Donald J. Trump as President of the United States. With these key victories, the newly emerged nationalists were positioned to challenge the status quo as well as global elites at most every turn.

I feel it is important to look at this issue from both perspectives. The ongoing struggle could impact and result in more convulsive environments in the coming decades as

---

[44] John G. Ruggie, "Multinationals as Global Institution: Power, Authority, and Relative Autonomy," Wiley Online Library, June 2017, https://onlinelibrary.wiley.com/doi/abs/10.1111/rego.12154.

skirmishes are fought and battles are won and lost. The raging war will result in potentially devastating and even scorched-earth encounters, with large swaths of people caught in between with little to do but ride the tides and ensuing chaos as best they can.[45]

FOR GLOBALIZATION

The disparity or gulf between those for and against globalization is as stark as between the most divisive political philosophies and structures. These competing theories and frameworks are at odds with little chance of reconciliation. The best we can hope for is a balancing of interests, which can lead to a partial truce between these two entrenched and ideologically divergent forces.

Those who support globalization trust in global citizenship and structures, believing the problems of humanity are too complex and large for individual nations to solve and thus are best resolved via more encompassing and sophisticated global structures.[46] Additionally, this form of globalism is based on the premise that all people are equal and all people matter, regardless of their heritage, race, or where they live or originate from.

---

45 Steven M. Gillon, "Why Populism in America is a Double-Edged Sword," History.com, February 2019, https://www.history.com/news/why populism-in-america-is-a-double-edged-sword.

46 Alvin Carpio, "The Answer to Nationalist Fervor Isn't Less Globalization. It's More," *World Economic Forum* (January 2019), https://www.weforum.org/agenda/2019/01/the-answer-to-nationalist-fervour-isnt-less-globalism-its-more/#:~:text=The%20answer%20to%20nationalist%20fervour%20isn't%20less%20globalism.,the%20people%20of%20the%20world.

Globalists further believe in a foundation of universal human rights that should be fostered and supported by all nation-states. These individuals and groups gravitate toward civic globalism, believing that thinking globally and acting locally provides the best opportunity to effect positive change around the world.[47]

AGAINST GLOBALIZATION

The arguments against globalization are equally grand and to the point. Those on this side of the issue feel that borders matter, and that cultural identity and community matter. They ultimately fear loss of national and cultural identity as well as political control of their fates and regions, with their needs and concerns subjugated to larger, more global needs, interests, and desires.

As noted, the term *globalist* has been utilized as a pejorative term to describe out-of-control leftists and cosmopolitans who favor internationalist projects and concerns over national interests. Populist leaders such as Donald Trump have weaponized this terminology to project and deflect blame and anger on such forces and peoples, laying responsibility for national issues and problems at the feet of globalism.[48]

Anti-globalist forces have also been accused of utilizing such larger macro issues to move forward their own narrow and even racist viewpoints. The nationalism/globalism debate has

---

[47] Kumi Naidoo, "The New Civic Globalism," *The Nation* (May 2000), https://www.thenation.com/article/archive/new-civic-globalism/.

[48] Liam Stack, "Globalism: A Far-Right Conspiracy Theory Buoyed by Trump," *The New York Times* (November 14, 2016), https://www.nytimes.com/2016/11/15/us/politics/globalism-right-trump.html.

quickly become one of the significant enablers and accelerants of the great cultural and political divides which we will discuss at a later point in this work.

Much has been laid bare and played out internationally with the recent Brexit vote and Great Britain's exit from the EU. Much of the rational behind this exit was thought to have, at its core, the inability of countries, particularly England, to control their borders and immigration policies.[49]

OPPORTUNITIES, CHALLENGES, AND LESSONS LEARNED

OPPORTUNITIES

While we seem to be at a precarious juncture currently, it is hard to imagine a scenario where globalism is not a dynamic part of our social and economic environment. There will be convulsions, dissension, and much political turmoil and debate, but ultimately globalism will prevail.

The entrenched and powerful forces propelling it forward simply will not be denied. Hopefully, those same forces will work with national political leaders to find a balance that is as equitable and sustainable as possible in the coming decades.

CHALLENGES

Politics is too unpredictable and seemingly unmanageable on a national scale. It is multitudes worse on a global scale,

---

49 "The Refugee Crisis, Brexit, and the Reframing of Immigration in Britain," *Europe Now Commentary* (June 2016), https://www.europenowjournal.org/2019/09/09/the-refugee-crisis-brexit-and-the-reframing-of-immigration-in-britain/.

as we have seen with trade agreements and climate accords. These unwieldy political and structural challenges can seem daunting if not impossible to overcome. As populist movements and leaders sporadically take hold in countries and regions of the world, reasonable proposals and conversations seem less likely to control the landscape, as opportunistic leaders enrage constituencies with misdirection and even lies.

Historical conflicts and geopolitical rivalries will also make it increasingly difficult to manage global growth and cooperation in ways we would desire or that would seem appropriate. Leaders and countries will have ambitions and agendas that seem bent on keeping entire populations wedged apart and at odds on important issues—ones that would seemingly lend them to much-needed collaboration and cooperation.

LESSONS LEARNED

The ultimate lessons learned are threefold. First, humans will not be contained or constrained. One way or another, we will find ways to experience and have the opportunities that global scale and structures provide.

Next, while politics are challenging and messy, solutions eventually have to be attained via our governing structures for lasting solutions to emerge. This will take time, and we will likely have to do (seemingly) everything wrong before we finally refocus our efforts and move in more appropriate and productive directions.

Finally, we collectively learn, solve problems, and work toward solutions, although not usually in a timely or efficient manner. We will need to show patience and determination, thinking in terms of centuries (not decades) in regard to many of the most complicated solutions and problems.[50]

We will likely have to hit the wall many times before we finally learn, evaluate, and adjust course. This was the case with the world wars, and it will likely be the case for many of the world's biggest challenges to come. Climate change, terrorism, immigration, and world health issues that will require efforts of global scale and structures to provide for meaningful and sustainable solutions.

---

[50] Mark Kramer, Marc Pfitzer, and Helge Mahne, "How Global Leaders Should Think About Solving Our Biggest Problems," HBR.com, January 2020, https://hbr.org/2020/01/how-global-leaders-should-think-about-solving-our-biggest-problems.

6 KEY TAKEAWAYS: GLOBALIZATION

1. Despite the tug of war between the nationalists and the globalists, there is no going back. Globalization will continue to increase in influence.
2. Globalism provides too many incentives and potential gains to be denied.
3. Transportation, technology, and communication will continue to serve as the ultimate foundations and facilitators of globalism.
4. Globalism stands as the best hope for raising standards of living of developing countries as well as entire regions around the world.
5. Many problems and issues are global in nature and must be attacked by more globalized structures and alliances.
6. Globalism is fueled by human ambition. This spirit and drive will not be contained.

4

THE FOURTH EVOLUTION: THE EXPLOSION OF TECHNOLOGICAL AND FINANCIAL SOPHISTICATION

Straub/Researcher: You mentioned that you are concerned about losing your job as a taxi driver to technology … could you elaborate?

Research Participant: On two fronts. One is just general change due to convenience, which is with Uber. The other to technology, which is in regard to artificial intelligence.

Straub/Researcher: Tell me about Uber and its threat to your job.

Research Participant: Well … they just have a great business concept, and they are starting to exploit the advantages.

It is a move to the gig economy. I have friends and relatives that are doing this part-time in other cities, possibly some in Cleveland that are scared to let me know.

People are doing this part-time, paying for the kids' college, or just getting out of debt. Works great for them.

But for people trying to make a full-time living in this line of work, it is becoming very difficult.

At least I am not in New York City. Those guys up there that bought those medallions are screwed. I have a friend who is in that city, and it is ugly. The city is trying to fight it [the Uber movement] ... but it is "death by a thousand cuts." They are going to eventually lose.

Straub/Researcher: Tell me your concerns about the technology threats that you referred to.

Research Participant: Well, that is the self-driving cars. They are already testing them out—not just cars either, over-the-road trucks ... possibly even delivery trucks eventually.

Straub/Researcher: Do you really feel this is a legitimate threat?

Research Participant: Absolutely ... just a matter of time.

Straub/Researcher: What is your plan in the face of all of this?

Research Participant: My son and I are already looking at starting our own company and throwing in with Uber. If you can't beat them, join them, right?

Straub/Researcher: What about the self-driving cars?

Research Participant: Not sure ... hopefully a human driver can add enough value to stay relevant. But the guys that just drive and don't talk and get to know their customers, their needs and patterns, are probably going to be gone. Maybe me too, who knows?

Researcher Note: *Five years after this interview, this driver and his son did start a three-car business (plus one limousine). They work with Uber, are doing well, and love working within that organizational structure.*

Historical movements and breakthroughs in our environments have facilitated and even necessitated dramatic gains in technological development. There is no better example than the 2019 outbreak and global transmission of the coronavirus known as COVID-19. This pandemic brought about a global effort for vaccines on a scale never witnessed before. There will no doubt be many more advancements necessitated by this global health event, impacting not only medicine and science but also many other aspects of our regular and economic lives

In this section of the book, we will examine various types of technological developments that will influence societies and economies as well as the general landscape. We will further examine some of the ways such advancements might impact both the macro and micro level of our lives, careers, and economies moving forward.

Out of the numerous innovations and growing sophistication, our goal will be to highlight a few of the most impactful changes to major workings of our society and economy. Medicine, technology, and finance are three areas we predict will be particularly significant in regard to continued and anticipated convulsive environments and events.

MEDICAL ADVANCES AND INNOVATION

There will be three notable expanses in the exploration of medical advances and innovation. First will be continued research and mapping of the human genome. This will spur designer drugs, manufactured body parts, and even improved genetics. All, of course, to those who have access to these wondrous new advancements.

This brings us to the second noteworthy issue in regard to medical advancement, that of access to and affordability of health care itself. With no realistic signs that costs will abate or reduce, the primary mechanism of accessing health care will be private or public insurance. The fight between private and/or public options will drag on continuously, with political parties and aligned interests attempting to sell the public on best possible solutions and potential outcomes.

This battle between philosophies and ideologies will result in a high-stakes tug of war, even a scorched-earth fight, leaving many individuals in its wake dealing with an increasingly uncertain, ill-defined landscape. This uncertainty will likely lead to a complicated, changing, and cumbersome patchwork of plans and regulations that will threaten the comprehensive care that many have grown accustomed to.[51]

With all this as our backdrop, there will be yet a third complication to withstand: the fight over vaccines. With the divergence of scientific opinion, more are choosing to forgo the normal (once accepted) regimens of vaccines. Further, with the 2019–20 pandemic, many have become disillusioned with

[51] Kimberly Amadeo, "Why Do We Need to Reform U.S. Health Care?" The Balance.com, October 2020, https://www.thebalance.com/why-reform-health-care-3305749.

the politicization of the science behind potential inoculations and therapies. Through this confusion and disinformation, it is possible the human race could lose long-fought battles against once-eradicated deceases like polio, mumps, and rubella.[52]

ROBOTICS AND ARTIFICIAL INTELLIGENCE

Robotics and artificial intelligence (AI) have burst on the scene and to the forefront of our consciousness and economy in the past two decades. There are two very distinct issues concerning these advanced technologies. The first is in relation to, can we manage and conquer the mechanics of such technological advancements? The second is a bit more nuanced and addresses the issue of how fast we can and should move in the directions these developments will likely take us. Answering the first is a bit easier; it deals with the actual skills and knowledge in play (all very definable) and the pace of change that is attainable. The second is much more difficult and controversial, as it deals with how beneficial such technologies are for society, economies, and the overall quality of our lives.

What makes the second question so problematic and complex is that the answer depends on who you ask and from what perspective the issue is approached. Is it beneficial? And if so, for who? There are obviously many titans of technology and industry lined up at the trough and feeding with abandon. There are huge sums to be made (billions) and many more advancements to come (resulting in even more billions).

---

[52] Shannon Bond, "The Perfect Storm: How Vaccine Misinformation Spread to the Mainstream," NPR.org, December 2020, https://www.npr.org/2020/12/10/944408988/the-perfect-storm-how-coronavirus-spread-vaccine-misinformation-to-the-mainstrea.

But as we look at the issue from the other side of the spectrum, things and perspectives can change very quickly. What will be the outcome of such massive technological advances, the net positives and negatives for society and economies as a whole? Again, it depends on who you ask and their perspective. Are they well educated? What is their age? Their adaptability to change? Their support networks? Bottom line, the number of perspectives and outlooks on these two developments will be substantial. Each individual has a different idea as to what advancements should take place and the most beneficial pace of those changes.

In some ways, the hand-wringing and discussion are irrelevant. There may be no way to change the speed of development or pace of change; while many argue the pace of tech growth is slowing somewhat, it will still serve as a test for individual people, careers, and entire industries to keep pace.[53] The best we may be able to do is to develop training and support systems to help those eventually effected, even displaced by these technologies. There are substantial and ongoing efforts in this regard, and no doubt they will continue moving forward.

The ultimate question is whether we can (or even have the will to) keep pace with such changes and help those most impacted. There will be efforts; we will develop rules, regulations, and infrastructure to help us contain the pace and direction. But in the end, it could prove futile, there being too many possibilities and variables to be slowed or denied.

The best that can happen is understanding at both the micro and macro level what is coming; identifying threats to

---

[53] Wad Roush, "Despite What You Might Think, Major Technological Changes Are Coming More Slowly Than They Once Did," *Scientific American* (August 2019), https://www.scientificamerican.com/article/despite-what-you-might-think-major-technological-changes-are-coming-more-slowly-than-they-once-did/.

jobs and careers as quickly and accurately as possible; and then positioning our economic systems accordingly. Governmental and educational resources can be marshaled in an effort to diminish the negative effects and consequences to life and career prospects.[54]

GROWING FINANCIAL SOPHISTICATION AND INCREASING LEVERAGE

It is of grave concern that present-day usage of debt and leverage are reaching unsustainable heights both nationally and globally. Individually, most have experience with debt and credit and the appropriate levels and uses of such tools. However, recent events involving housing and the looming student-loan debt crisis have shown that individuals struggle to find the balance in relation to dealing with personal debt and credit utilization. The same can be said in regard to the macro level and utilization of large-scale national and global debt. Many countries seem similarly inept at managing growing debt levels.[55]

The primary reason this is emerging as a crisis is the ineffective structures of constitutions and other governmental structures, both national and global. Most provide little systemic constraint on leverage and allow for runaway debts and deficits to continue unabated.[56] While the 2008 debt crisis should have

54 Andrew Stettner, "There's Already a US Program That Could Help Workers Who Lose Their Jobs to Machines," Quartz.com, April 2018, https://qz.com/work/1265821/theres-a-us-trade-program-that-could-help-workers-who-lose-their-jobs-to-ai/.

55 "Be Informed: National Debt," Just Facts.com, https://www.justfacts.com/nationaldebt.asp.

56 Henry J. Aaron, "Constitutional Solutions to Our Escalating National Debt: Examining Balanced Budget Amendments," Brookings.edu, July 2014, https://www.brookings.edu/testimonies/

served as a national and global wakeup call, highlighting the dangers of our over-leveraged financial institutions and lax regulation of business and governmental structures, it seems to have provided minimal education, and any lessons learned seem to have faded quickly.

The utilization of debt and credit (at unsustainable levels) would seem to be a looming un-voted-upon transfer of wealth from future generations to current generations, with little constraint or oversight. What does this mean in regard to what follows? It seems very possible that instability and uncertainty will proliferate. Convulsions could grow greater and more compressed when governments and economies are forced to deal with the reality of such debts and deficits.

There are three very painful ways to deal with these issues: increased taxes, reduced spending, and/or inflation. While the final option—countries inflating their way out of problems—might seem tempting, even desirable, there are a host of problems and issues associated with such a strategy. In reality, it serves as a un-voted-upon tax on all citizens. Additionally, it presents a substantial issue in the form of moral hazard. Once governments (and citizens) have utilized this tool to solve current problems, what is to stop them from doing it again and again?

Initiating such actions and processes could entice more individuals and entities to utilize alternative payment schemes, such as bartering and cryptocurrencies, potentially sidestepping governmental taxing structures altogether. Finally, if taxes escalate substantially, the wealthiest and most liquid will take their gains and move elsewhere in search of lower taxes

---

constitutional-solutions-to-our-escalating-national-debt-examining-balanced-budget-amendments/.

and more favorable conditions. Those without such liquidity, wealth, and prospects will be left holding the proverbial bag.

OPPORTUNITIES, CHALLENGES, AND LESSONS LEARNED

OPPORTUNITIES

While we have highlighted the immense complications and challenges posed by the pace and growth of technological change and financial sophistication, there is no doubt that there are many associated opportunities as well.

First is the utilization of technology to facilitate opportunity, efficiency, and effectiveness. Barriers to learning and access to education that used to exist have been batted down at lightning speed via online learning and the new educational delivery competencies—some gained via the pandemic. The robotics and artificial intelligence that seem at first glance to be so ominous can be utilized to eliminate mundane and even dangerous tasks, making workplaces safer and more fulfilling.

Next, medical advances will allow for longer life spans and better quality of life, nationally and globally. We must utilize our skills and sophisticated talents to make such tools and advancements available and affordable to more individuals. Gains have been made by NGOs like the Gates Foundation and many others to improve such access and effectiveness around the world.[57]

---

[57] Nahaly Nafisa Khan, "Digital Transformation in the Health Sector: Making Healthcare More Inclusive and Accessible," *The Daily Star* (February 2021), https://www.thedailystar.net/supplements/30th-anniversary-supplements/going-digital/news/digital-transformation-the-health-sector-making-healthcare-more-inclusive-and-accessible.

Additionally, the tools of debt and leverage ultimately allow us to even out the bumps and dangers in irregular economic cycles. These financial strategies that currently seem so toxic and dangerous can also serve as wondrous tools for humanity if utilized in appropriate and responsible ways.

Finally, globalization can and will be an astounding and continually sustainable tool for humanity to share opportunities and transfer skills around the planet. It will be incumbent on us to isolate and develop better governance structures to help deal with the many trials that will result from such movement and ambitions.

CHALLENGES

While we have already talked about some of the challenges that could potentially face us in the wake of such momentous forces, there are two others that bear mentioning.

First, there is a greater opportunity to spread mischief and misinformation. New tools like deep fake technologies will make it ever more difficult to ascertain what is real and what is not. This confusion and misdirection will make it increasingly easy to spread misperception and dissension in regions and entire countries, hijacking political elections and turning entire populations against each other.

Next, as noted previously is the lack of constraints in many countries and regions on leverage and deficit spending. This reality, left unchecked, could lead to intergenerational looting of resources and opportunities on a scale unimaginable to the founding fathers and designers of our constitutional structures and foundations.

LESSONS LEARNED

At the writing of this first edition, it seems the verdict is out on what has been learned in regard to much of what has been highlighted and discussed. While we remain hopeful, it seems that we are currently stuck in a social and cultural doom loop of missed opportunity, drama, and chaos.

As noted, we have tremendous opportunities and incredible tools at our disposal. What remains to be seen is whether we have the discipline, will, and mechanisms in place to marshal our societies, cultures, and political structures in constructive ways and directions.

If we pay attention to history, it is evident how easy it is to distract entire populations with the macabre, convenient, and entertaining to keep them from focusing on what's important. The ancient Romans accomplished it with the gruesome and brutal displays in the Colosseum; our leaders, nefarious actors, and elites currently accomplish much of the same with political manipulation and deception as well as the general spectacle of politics, sports and entertainment.

6 KEY TAKEAWAYS: TECHNOLOGICAL AND FINANCIAL SOPHISTICATION

1. Technological sophistication will continue to grow exponentially.
2. Robotics and artificial intelligence will potentially disrupt jobs, businesses, and entire industries.
3. Technological advances will continue to drive increased medical advances and life expectancy (to those with access).
4. All governments will be tasked with knocking through the hyperbolic irrationality and identifying sensible and sustainable solutions.
5. COVID-19 will drive better communication and cooperation, attempting to tamp down on potential and future pandemic threats.
6. Governments will need to develop more effective financial strategies and models to encourage more intergenerational financial stability and sustainability.

5

THE FIFTH EVOLUTION: THE GREAT DIVIDE AND THE POST-TRUTH WORLD

Research Participant: I'm just too damned old! Nobody wants to hire me.

Straub/Researcher: What about legal and regulatory protections?

Research Participant: They're not supposed to discriminate, but they do. They look at your résumé, and they can sort it all out … do the math. I worked my whole career in human resources … I know how it all works.

Worst part is … I used to do the same thing to other people that I am bitching about now—exactly the same thing. Not so amusing when it's happening to you.

Straub/Researcher: What is your current situation?

Research Participant: I got tossed out of my job after twenty-seven years. I am fifty-five years old … I feel I still can do the job.

I've kept up, pretty current. Not afraid to learn. I know I probably can't make what I was before; I'll take less if they will just give me a chance.

Half the time, I am interviewing with some kid that could be my child … if I get lucky enough to get an interview.

You can see the look in their eye … arrogance, even disrespect at times. They think you are a dinosaur.

I mean, what are we going to do with all these people? Many don't have enough money to retire … we have to do something! Have to work!

My kids try to help at times … but they have their own problems.

Straub/Researcher: How do you feel at this time?

Research Participant: Desperate, pissed, scared … What the hell happened to this country, the American Dream? Nothing works anymore!

When examining the topic of the great divide and the post-truth world, we might at first be tempted to put it in the classification of a fad or a temporary state of disrepair in regard to our societal and cultural landscape. There are several reasons why I feel it is much more serious and demands to be categorized as its own evolution.

If you look through the lens of history, you will see that these divisions are not simply recent phenomenon. These same polarizing forces have been at work since the early ages of human existence. There have always been those who would divide and conquer, utilizing fear and prejudice to entice populations to do unimaginable, even horrific things to one another.

The difference at this point in history is that there has never been a more opportune time and more effective, even lethal, tools to distract, destroy, and confuse the larger population.[58] The everyday tools provided by technology and social media—including sophisticated devices like AI, spying through listening devices, and deep fake videos—allow those with means, ambitions, and opportunity to manipulate large swaths of people and push our predictable and easily accessible buttons.

THE HISTORY OF POLARIZATION

As noted, despite a somewhat convenient narrative, polarization is not new. In fact, it is ongoing, to be expected, and old as humanity itself. There are glaringly obvious examples, such as the US Civil War. Such division also happens in the realm of business, politics, religion, and every other endeavor that has large accumulations of people within organized environments.

Furthermore, in the scope of hundred-to thousand-year blocks of recorded history, polarization and division can even be viewed as positive and resulting in long-term, even sustainable growth for societies, cultures, and regions. Finally, it could be argued that without such divergence, society, political discourse, and nations would become stagnate and eventually weaken.

---

[58] Thomas Carothers and Andrew O'Donohue, "Democracies Divided—The Global Challenge of Political Polarization," Brookings Institution Press (2019), https://carnegieendowment.org/2019/10/01/how-to-understand-global-spread-of-political-polarization-pub-79893.

So while the process can and usually will be chaotic and uncomfortable, these types of division and polarization are in reality a necessity to move debate and communal growth forward. With that said, polarization can also decimate and destroy organizations and even entire countries that wind up on the scrap heap of history due to uncontrolled and overly divisive forces.

So how can we find the correct balance? Is such equilibrium attainable? Finally, how has that balance and equilibrium been impacted as a result of the increased growth and expansion of technology? What makes this topic so pesky and complex is the sheer nature of its characterization. I will highlight six areas that will continue to challenge us and add an exponentiality to this emergent phenomenon.

GLOBALISM VS. NATIONALISM

We have touched on this issue previously, but it warrants further discussion within this context. The issue surrounding the predominance of globalist vs. nation-state governmental structures is and will be with us for the foreseeable future. There are significant forces on both sides of this deliberation that wield considerable clout and resources and will deploy them aggressively.

The process is turning into a scorched-earth battle, with neither side willing to relent or give any ground to the other. The two sides seem to have well-staked-out and opposing positions, much like the polarity witnessed on such issues as abortion and other divisive social issues.

The inertia seemed to be in favor of the globalists, with free-trade agreements gaining momentum, the advent of the

European Union, and the free flow of travel and education. However, in more recent times, dissatisfaction among specific classes of people (predominantly middle and lower) have fueled the rise of populist leaders in the United States, Europe, and other regions of the world. The inevitability of a new globalist structure and hierarchy seems now to be in a state of transition and uncertainty.

In fact, the role of the United States as the long-standing policeman and enforcer of world order seems in jeopardy, and at the very least in a state of transition. The rise of populist leaders in the Republican ranks has called this long-held role into question, with many preferring an America First policy and more introspective view of the US role in world affairs. With the United States seeming to waver or even vacate this long-held and crucial global role, other players, namely Russia and China, are moving in to fill the void.[59]

With the United Kingdom leaving the European Union, and the supremacy of the United Nations, the World Health Organization, and other NGOs being challenged, it seems obvious the dissenting forces are gaining a foothold and additional influence.[60] In light of the COVID-19 pandemic, the debate is even more open to differing viewpoints. More people, corporations, and entire governments are now questioning their previous assumptions in regard to global philosophies and structures.

---

[59] "Populism in the United States: A Timeline," History.com, December 2018, https://www.history.com/topics/us-politics/populism-united-states-timeline.

[60] "Europe and Right-Wing Nationalism: A Country-by-Country Guide," BBCNews.com, November 2019, https://www.bbc.com/news/world-europe-36130006.

THE PREEMINENCE OF SCIENCE

The long-held belief in the preeminence of science is being questioned regularly in our fractured environment. Despite assertions that the science is settled on a laundry list of matters, there remains dissension and controversy at every turn.

Long-accepted issues, such as vaccines, are now controversial, with politicians, celebrities, and thought leaders all jumping into the fray on both sides. This newfound and amplified skepticism has been on full display during the 2020 global pandemic, as valuable time has been lost debating the efficacy and trustworthiness of scientific thought and the advice of leading health professionals and national institutions.[61]

The battle over climate change and its legitimacy has been tossed, turned, and derailed via challenges to scientific theory and academic research on the phenomenon. Further confusing the issue are select scientists willing to take positions based on pseudo-science funded by wealthy and aligned interests, making it more difficult for the people trying to identify reality and position accordingly.[62]

ECONOMIC ENTITLEMENT AND OPPORTUNITY

With progressively more focus on the issues surrounding equality and social justice, the foundations and assumptions of our capitalist structure have come under increasing scrutiny and assault. A divide over equality of opportunity and privileged

[61] Chris Mooney, "The Science of Why We Don't Believe Science," MotherJones.com, May/June 2011, https://www.motherjones.com/politics/2011/04/denial-science-chris-mooney/.

[62] Mooney, "The Science of Why We Don't Believe Science."

status garnered via race, gender, and birthright have dominated discussions within families, communities, and political parties.

The traditional structures rewarding connections, education, and meritocracy are discussed and increasingly questioned, scrutinizing foundational and institutional structures that benefit some and constrain others. Several forceful and aligned groups are demanding equal access and even demanding redistributive social justice for the sins of previous generations. This tug of war is on full display in current battles between progressives, moderates and conservatives within political parties and structures worldwide. Activist demonstrations by groups such as Occupy Wall Street and the Capital Hill Autonomous Zone in Seattle have taken these debates to new and more intense levels via civil disobedience and even direct violation of laws and property rights.

CULTURAL POLARITIES

The cultural polarities are on full display on a variety of issues ranging from social to economic. The substantial red state/blue state divide in the United States is built on fault lines predominantly based on urban versus rural regions, with their defined and divergent political ideologies.[63] Along with the structural and geographic divides are disagreements on the concept of patriotism itself, as well as the definition of what it means to be a country or a citizen.

Closely tied to the rural and urban fracture is the issue of

---

[63] Josh Kron, "Red State, Blue City: How the Urban-Rural Divide Is Splitting America," TheAtlantic.com, November 2012, https://www.theatlantic.com/politics/archive/2012/11/red-state-blue-city-how-the-urban-rural-divide-is-splitting-america/265686/.

Second Amendment (gun) rights. Should there be such rights, and what are the limitations to such freedoms? I think most agree the Second Amendment is an important part of our constitutional structure, but the larger and more divisive issue surrounds what the definition of gun rights should be and, more importantly, the privileges, freedoms, and boundaries of such liberties.

While much of the debate regarding the supremacy of science is again centered somewhat on such widening cultural divides, additional controversy is founded on an even more wide-ranging debate, that of a more secular society versus the more traditional religious foundations of our nation. Closely associated are controversial and divisive topics like abortion and marriage rights, as well as sexual identification. Throw into this climate racial and gender tensions recently heightened by events leading to the Black Lives Matter as well as the #me-too movement, and it makes for a complicated and toxic environment.[64]

Further complicating this cultural confusion are vast disagreements in regard to what constitutes both history and fact. In an age when any individual can backfill seemingly legitimate facts via a plethora of aligned and compromised information sources, there is more confusion than ever about what constitutes a fact or what embodies the truth.

I suspect this will get even more complicated as historians increasingly align with political and special-interest groups, much like political pollsters, in essence manufacturing designer history that panders to a particular ideology and sanctioned

---

64 "Americas Biggest Issues—The Top Issues Facing Our Nation," Heritage.org, https://www.heritage.org/americas-biggest-issues?gclid=CjwKCAiAsaOBBhA4EiwAo0_AnGsmNIkyydII3qz0XE0O6Ov8e9qpRCDSCsP0vlJdoeLzq-V1nP4f9xoCjIcQAvD_BwE.

alternate reality. We further anticipate that red-state and blue-state educational systems, particularly K through 12, will order textbooks from those authors and publishers that align with their world view and political ideologies (regarding, for example, the Civil War, January 6 Capital attack and social issues). This potential divergence of reality could lead to even more confusion, disagreement, and confrontation than ever before as we move away from a collective interpretation of American history.

THE ROLE OF GOVERNMENT

Much current controversy and political debate centers on the desired and required role of governments in our societies, with two well-funded and well-organized groups facing off in this ideological fight. Both are closely aligned with the structures of the two major political parties. Individuals, believing government is the answer to most problems, predominantly align with the progressive wing of the Democratic Party. The less-is-more conservative and even libertarian factions that believe in free trade, little to no regulation, and free enterprise associate themselves closely with the far right and Tea Party wings of the Republican Party.

Both groups are affiliated with and funded by activist donors and supporters such as the Koch's on the far right and George Soros on the far left, among many others. This high-stakes battle is fueled by an explosion of money into campaigns throughout the country (via the Citizens United ruling, 2010). At stake are state and national legislatures, governorships, and even the presidency of the United States.[65] Such electoral gains are the ultimate prize for such backers, leading to the most coveted prize of all—the designation of federal and Supreme Court judgeships.

The stakes are incredibly high, and many states continue to see regional and statewide elections hijacked by such high-powered donors and activist groups. This reality makes many wonder if these elected officials are loyal to their local constituencies or the moneyed elitists who paid for their campaigns and ultimately their victories. Like many other of the great-divide issues, this one will likely be in dispute for some time to come.

POLITICAL STRUCTURES AND THE TWO-PARTY SYSTEM

Finally, we get to the most prevalent tool of division in our current environment: political party structures. This divisiveness has been fueled by a number of issues, but chief among them are two pervasive challenges: the age of the professional politician and the severe lack of constraints on our political system to prevent money and influence from dominating the political landscape.

To clarify, I define *professional politicians* as those who utilize political positions as their sole or primary source of income and career progress, as opposed to a citizen politician who uses this as a secondary sources of income and career

[65] David M. Shribman, "Ten Years On, Citizens United Ruling Has Changed U.S. Politics—But Not in the Way Many Feared," latimes.com, January 2020, https://www.latimes.com/world-nation/story/2020-01-12/citizens-united-ruling-anniversary-how-it-changed-american-politics.

while maintaining a full-time primary source of income. To further illustrate, it is not uncommon for national politicians in our current environment to never work outside the beltway. Many work for lobbies or DC law firms before and after leaving political office.[66]

Next, we get to the two-party structure, with its closed primary systems and the ultimate tool of entrenched party structures: gerrymandering. The primary processes are increasingly dominated by the far wings of the parties, each coalescing around social and cultural issues that drive volunteerism and passion, such as abortion rights, gun rights, and gay marriage, as well as racial, immigration, and sexual-identity issues. Candidates throughout the primary process are controlled and cajoled by such groups; they are graded and forced to pass purity tests at every juncture. By the time candidates get through the process, they have been pulled so far to the extremes that those voting in the general elections find it difficult to identify with either candidate offering.

This process has eradicated moderates from both parties, leaving them hat-in-hand without so much as a big-tent sales pitch as they are summarily shown the door.[67] This process has cemented the control of the two-party system, but to make it official, party leaders on both sides have shown unity and bipartisanship in one respect: the wondrous tool of gerrymandering.

The process of *gerrymandering*, or of letting party insiders conveniently and strategically divide up regions and districts to assure a high number of under- or even uncontested races, leads

---

66 Jonathan Rauch, "How American Politics Went Insane," theatlantic.com, July/August 2016, https://www.theatlantic.com/magazine/archive/2016/07/how-american-politics-went-insane/485570/.

67 Rauch, "How American Politics Went Insane."

to marginalization and lack of political opportunity for the masses.[68] Some states have fought this trend, but the majority have allowed the political parties to impose their will and have their way with the election landscape.

Finally, the structure of the electoral process itself is hugely controversial at the present time, particularly the Electoral College, the system that the founders put in place to save us from ourselves and our worst tendencies.[69] Putting yet another check and balance against our impetuous natures and inflamed passions, this tool has recently influenced two of the most controversial elections in the past two decades: Bush vs. Gore and Clinton vs. Trump. Many fear there are more to come in the decades ahead, as our divisiveness grows and razor-thin popular-vote margins prevail.

OPPORTUNITIES, CHALLENGES, AND LESSONS LEARNED

OPPORTUNITIES

While politics and the political environment are ugly, brutish, and even counterproductive at times, it is only through the political process that we can take on the most significant challenges and problems of the day. So it is in this light that we will optimistically view the cup as half full and discuss the opportunities of the current environment.

---

68 Will Rahn, "How Gerrymandering Became One of the Biggest Issues in Politics," cbsnews.com, March 2019, https://www.cbsnews.com/news/how-gerrymandering-became-one-of-the-biggest-issues-in-politics/.

69 "What Is the Electoral College and Why Is it Controversial?" Adl.com, https://www.adl.org/education/resources/tools-and-strategies/what-is-the-electoral-college-and-why-is-it-controversial.

Initially, I would highlight that votes and voters can make a difference. They can make their voices heard, even over the megaphones of the politicians themselves as well as the money and influence associated with the process.

It cannot be ignored that the candidacies of Donald Trump and Bernie Sanders in 2016 were in some ways different sides of the same coin. While it is obvious the two candidates could not be more different ideologically, they did have one major thing in common: they were the electorate's tools to send a very strong and loud message to the political establishment—a metaphorical double bird, if you will—letting it know that people were tired of business as usual in their political structures and ways of doing business. Both Trump and Sanders were a direct and successful challenge (drain the swamp) to the Clintons, the Bushes, and the seeming stranglehold of entrenched interests on the two-party system.

That being said, both Sanders and Trump affiliated with the major party systems to push for such reform. While it was obviously an uneasy marriage for both the parties and the candidates, in our current system and structure, it was absolutely the necessary solution.

That being said, both candidates proved that with charisma and incredible force of will, large and disruptive change can be made to the political landscape. While neither probably saw the ultimate changes he would have liked, they certainly left a transformed landscape and workable playbook for those who follow. These will certainly not be the last disruptors we will see in the political arena.

Politics at its core is still a noble endeavor. It allows people to affiliate, group up, and lobby their elected representatives for needed services as well as changes to governmental systems. Another optimistic note is that most acknowledge we share much in common, despite the fact that media sources, politicians, and moneyed interests effectively direct and manipulate us to focus on the small proportion of issues that wedge and divide us.

This commonality will hopefully and ultimately win the day. We will come to recognize and fight the forces that continue to separate us. One needed mechanism to accomplish this will be combating the amount of money pouring into races of all types and from areas and regions completely unassociated with many of the elections being contested.

CHALLENGES

There are numerous challenges that make sustainable change in our political structures difficult. First is our nature. We all like a good competition, and we have become increasingly desensitized to how personal and dirty it can get—even enjoying the carnage at times.

Next, many regions are becoming more diverse. While that has many advantages and opportunities, this diversity becomes a convenient opportunity for political forces to wedge us and even pit us against each other. Hot-button issues such as abortion rights, unions, religion, and gun rights will continue to be the gasoline poured on and inflaming such passions.

Additionally, there are many entrenched and powerful forces that are doing very well under the current structures and systems. The political parties themselves are at the top of this list. There is simply too much money allowed into the system. It is the mother's milk of politics, and professional politicians will do anything to maintain their lofty perch, finances, and perks.

Also, there will be a day of reckoning for our city, state, and federal budget deficits. This new age of limited resources will create pack mentalities as groups try to protect their pet projects and budget interests. This environment will be easily manipulated and exploited by politicians, parties, lobbyists, and other organizations seeking to accomplish their own goals.

Finally, all of this will happen and take place in a post-truth world of alternative facts, deep fakes, and outright lies and chicanery the likes of which we have never seen. This will be a combined assault led by foreign governments, our own political structures, and the media (both mainstream and social).

While there will be no shortage of dissatisfaction with the players, process, and structures that we have highlighted, there will also be no shortage of ideas and ways to fix the problems. It will likely be very difficult to find significant consensus. Therefore, the ultimate search for solutions could provide just as much drama and disagreement as the problems themselves.

LESSONS LEARNED

The good news is that we are learning and identifying the factors at play in this bold and somewhat menacing new world. Many are waking up to the manipulative forces around us, and more of us are attempting and committed to pulling free of these disreputable influences.

Some are working to learn of more reputable news and information sources that give us a more multidimensional and nuanced understanding of issues and challenges. Unfortunately, the saying that "necessity is the mother of invention" may hold prominence in this discussion. We may have further to fall and more to suffer before ultimately retaking control of our destinies and fortunes.

6 KEY TAKEAWAYS: THE GREAT DIVIDE

1. Campaign finance reform must be reviewed and reworked to tamp down on the historic amounts of money in the political realm.
2. The utilization of gerrymandering will need to be reviewed and reduced significantly to diminish the number of uncontested districts.
3. There is a needed emergence and importance of the moderate wings in each party. This could bring back a sense of fairness to the political landscape.
4. A move to nonpartisan or open primary systems, in which voters are not required to declare party affiliation, should be considered.
5. We need to find a more appropriate balance between freedom of speech and truthful, respectful discourse in the political arena.
6. We must all look at ourselves and assess our role in this great divide and do our best to help in bringing our cities, states, and nation back to common sense and common ground.

THE SECOND CONVULSION:
OUT OF THE FRYING PAN AND INTO THE FIRE

COMPONENTS OF 6E THINKING

- adaptability and toughness
- practicality
- strong and stable relationships
- scenario planning
- lifelong learning

While my father was dealing with the impending disruption to his job and career, he was also cultivating his long-cherished goal of achieving his entrepreneurial dreams and ambitions. He had harbored these desires since he was a young man, manifested early on with his experience of owning a small cattle herd while still a young adult.

The golden opportunity and dream of owning his own business would present itself via a call from a mentor and old friend he knew from the oil industry. This friend made my father and brother aware of a service company, a business that was struggling due to poor management. It would be a somewhat treacherous opportunity; they would need to partner (at least initially) with the individual who was running the business into such troubled circumstances. But this friend was sure there was a significant opportunity, and that if they were not able to work with their fledgling partner, they would eventually have the potential to extricate him from the business via a buyout.

With their wherewithal and financial resources, my father and my brother Ron embarked on what would turn into a successful multi-decade journey through the business and entrepreneurial landscape. As expected, the industry opportunity was lucrative; and, as suspected, it was not possible to work with the existing partner, who proved to be too unstable and erratic. My father and brother were compelled to buy him out after four years and move forward with the company. Now they were in complete control of the business and their future prospects.

The business was renamed under the Straub banner, initially as Straub Oilfield Services. Later, it would be renamed and rebranded Straub International, Inc. Ron's wife, Kathy, was added to the business as an accountant and eventually become the company's Chief Financial Officer. Her financial expertise and the team's management acumen would be desperately needed, as the company faced several challenges in the decade ahead.

While the business fared well throughout the first seven or eight years, ultimately it was not to last. The great oil bust of the late 1970s and entire decade of the 1980s would pose very real and threatening challenges to the young company. During this demanding period, and as the future looked very bleak, my father saw a classified ad in the local newspaper placed by International Harvester Company. The company was searching for an agricultural equipment dealer to replace a recently terminated agency (his former employer). He was intrigued.

He knew it could be a big risk and that his banker, wife, and family would need some convincing. While Wally was excited and ready to pounce on the opportunity, it could be argued that it was akin to jumping out of the fire (of the oil industry woes) and into the frying pan.

International Harvester Company was in perilous shape. There were regular articles about the company's uncertain future and distressed prospects. They were struggling due to high interest rates and poor management as well as the perilous prospects for their two primary products: trucks and agricultural equipment.

After much research, and much convincing and cajoling of the different stakeholders, it was decided that the young company would pursue the opening. Wally knew there was a lot of opportunity to be gained, but it would require skilled and expert employees to quickly move forward. Fortunately, he had good relationships and a sterling reputation with the former employees of his previous company, and he was able to staff up quickly and successfully.

Straub International, Inc., the reimagined business, was staffed, operational, and doing very well in its first two years of operations—until an unanticipated happening. In 1985, J. I. Case Corporation bought the struggling International Harvester Company's agricultural equipment division. Both had long traditions in the agriculture industry, and it was felt there would be many synergies gained via the proposed merger.

The problem was that the two companies had similar dealer footprints, and those would have to be rationalized, since they were merging the brands of the company into a unified Case IH equipment brand and organizational structure.

This issue and reality would result in the newly merged companies' dealer rationalization teams going across the country and meeting with and assessing dealers that were in the same markets. One dealer would get the assigned territory; the other would be bought out (and in most cases liquidated). We, along with dealers across the country, would wait anxiously to be informed of our outcome.

After six months, we were assessed and selected to be the dealer for our region. We were provided with inducements as well as lucrative financing to buy the non-surviving dealer out of the market area as well as its physical assets. The process went smoothly, and we found ourselves with a dramatically expanded product line and customer base, and a much stronger position in the marketplace.

However, due to the extended wait for the rationalization teams to arrive at our dealerships, I was faced with the prospect of possibly having to find another job and career pathway. It was at this point that I decided to relaunch my educational journey, beginning the work to finish my partially completed bachelor's degree.

PART TWO

THE 6IXTH EVOLUTION: LIVING IN AN AGE OF EXPONENTIAL CHANGE AND HYPER CONVULSIVE ENVIRONMENTS

The pace of change and the threat of disruption creates tremendous opportunities.—**Steve Case**

The whole system is under tremendous strain. Although the increasing pace of change is essential for developing new solutions, it is also pushing society to its limits. In global structures, it all comes to a head in the form of sudden crises. This leads to tipping point situations in which the seemingly impossible becomes possible.—**Franz Josef Radermacher**

6 WHAT IS BRINGING ABOUT THIS NEW AGE?

Employment Placement Professional: You know, it's interesting … I have been in the employment counseling and placement business for over two decades … and it is so striking to me … the difference in outcomes.

Straub/Researcher: How do you mean?

Employment Placement Professional: People talk a lot about ageism and discrimination … and it is a problem. No matter how many laws you pass, how many regulations … so many organizations are looking for younger and cheaper.

But, just like with automobiles … the condition of the product matters. There are fifty-year-olds, and there are "rode hard put away wet" fifty-year-olds. The people who are current, stay vibrant and in shape (physically and mentally), they are not that hard to place … Then there are the others.

Straub/Researcher: Can you elaborate?

Employment Placement Professional: People whose biological and intellectual age is more than their actual number. They are partially checked out; some were actually retired in place. They just stopped trying, stopped growing … their pilot light went out.

Worst part is, they don't have the retirement savings to quit … not even close. So they have to try to get re-employed … we have to try to assist them. It is a tough sell at times. Some pretty sad stories. People need to understand how important it is to stay in the game, to stay viable … to finish strong.

There are several theories in regard to what is bringing the realities we have highlighted to the forefront. I will address a few possibilities at this time. One involves the acknowledgement that human will and ambition will not be restrained. Another is the exponential growth of technological advancement. Finally, there is the reality that we are destined, even challenged to outrun ourselves; it is in our nature to push the limits of possibilities and curiosity, and we simply will not limit our capacity to do so.

While each of these is only part of the answer, I will address more comprehensive possibilities in this segment of the book. We will look at the key realms of our society and economy to provide clarity for this question.

POLITICAL

It is fitting that we start with our political environment, since this is timely and very close to the root of many current problems and issues. As per the focus of the book, we will key in on the American political arena, but many of the issues identified are applicable to political structures in many different countries.

The overall challenges and dysfunction of the American political system cannot be denied or overstated. While the founders did a very good job of putting together a political structure for their historical times, they simply could not have foreseen many of the contemporary developments that have come to pass—technological advancements, sociological and cultural change, and especially information platforms that could sow seeds of doubt, threatening our very democracy at the stroke of a key. I will highlight four key areas of governments and political structures that are key to the realities we face currently.

First is the structural flaws of our constitutional governing configurations. While we must give our founders a high passing grade for their initial work, there are quite simply major advances and progressions they could not have foreseen. Unfortunately, our Constitution is lumbering, unwieldy, and by design very difficult to change and reconfigure. In an age when we can barely muster a simple majority to elect many federal offices of the United States, it seems improbable that we can muster the supermajorities necessary to amend our US Constitution.[70]

[70] Scott Bomboy, "What Does It Take to Repeal a Constitution Amendment?" *Constitution Daily* (March 2018), https://constitutioncenter.org/blog/what-does-it-take-to-repeal-a-constitutional-amendment.

While this structure was put in place for a reason, there is no overstating the extreme challenge of getting the necessary consensus to amend our current structures. There is such distrust and negative discourse that we seem destined to navigate a twenty-first-century landscape with nineteenth-century transportation.

Second, the country's very polarized and highly dysfunctional political structures are unable to perform the basic (and required) functions of government. A primary function of our congress is the passing of yearly federal budgets. This has not been done successfully since 1996. Instead, Congress has resorted to massive omnibus appropriation bills and continuing resolutions that perpetuate bloated and ill-conceived budgets from year to year.[71] The two major political parties have a stranglehold on our national political landscape and use that advantage to shut all other potential parties out of government management and administration. Both parties utilize weapons like gerrymandering—and vast sums of political contributions—as their tools of choice to guarantee their long-term survival. Both parties work together in an unholy alliance to guarantee their political prospects at the expense of and overall success and sustainability of the country they were elected to serve.

Third is the dysfunctional structure of coequal branches of government (Congress, Presidency, and Judiciary). While we can understand why our founders found this type of structure desirable, this diffusing of power could hinder our ability to navigate tricky and convulsive environments. After fleeing the tyranny of the kings of Europe, the founders were reluctant to

[71] Gus Wezerek, "20 Years of Congress's Budget Procrastination, In One Chart," Five Thirty Eight, February 2018, https://fivethirtyeight.com/features/20-years-of-congresss-budget-procrastination-in-one-chart/.

put too much power in any one branch of government. They wished to have suitable and sufficient checks and balances for our governmental leaders.

But with tools such as the Senate filibuster and presidential impeachment proceedings being wielded like common weapons instead of the tools of last resort intended by our designers, our coequal structures now feels like a gridlocked and toothless giant rather than the agile and pliable instrument the founders initially might have envisioned.

Finally, what I refer to as the one that got away: the lack of a balanced budget amendment. This gaping hole in our constitutional structure allows a loophole for our population and political parties to co-opt each other and spend the resources of the country without sufficient checks, balances, or restraints. This has resulted in generational transfers of wealth that could leave future generations saddled with massive amounts of debts and deficits.[72]

While it is understandable that a federal government needs to have latitude for times of war and unforeseen and natural disaster, the complete lack of constraint and its results were probably never visualized or foreseen by our founding fathers.

SOCIAL AND CULTURAL

Key aspects of this domain have resulted in increasing levels of drama and controversy. These are all areas that can be (on the surface) more easily impacted than the Constitution-related

[72] Kimberly Amadeo, "Why US Deficit Spending Is Out of Control—Why Government Leaders Continue to Deficit Spend," The Balance, February 2021, https://www.thebalance.com/deficit-spending-causes-why-it-s-out-of-control-3306289.

realities just discussed, but they are nevertheless complicated, delicate, and multidimensional in their own right.

The foremost is information and communication flow in our societies and environments. The challenges encompass the entire landscape currently, from traditional media to social media and the even more disconcerting and nefarious residual actors, such as hostile countries and internet trolls.

Many of the traditional media sources have long ago traded their independence for profitable and cozy political and economic alliances, calling much of their content and reliability to increasing levels of scrutiny.[73] Social media outlets, both traditional and nontraditional, have increasingly dominated this content area with ambitious, aligned, and questionable agendas. Suspect interests (governments and other entities) around the world effectively and callously utilize such mediums to manipulate our electoral processes as well as stoke fear, suspicion, and outright division within our citizenry.

And standing by is a cadre of celebrities, entertainers, late-night hosts, and even athletes all very willing to jump into the fray, marshaling their legions of fans and supporters to enter the field of public opinion and battle. Much of this taking place with less and less civility, sometimes with outright hostility and vulgarity.

Some issues that are creating many of the cultural tensions in the landscape are decades, even centuries in the making. Issues of race and inequality have been simmering below the surface, many would argue, since the Civil War, especially coming to a head during the civil rights movement and more

---

[73] Jim Kuypers, "Partisan Journalism—A History of Media Bias in the United States," Rowman & Littlefield, 2014, https://www.amazon.com/Partisan-Journalism-History-Communication-Politics/dp/1442252073.

recently the Black Lives Matter effort.[74] Other more current movements, such as LGBTQ rights, have become significant in the past decades, picking up momentum particularly in recent years. Another more recent phenomenon is multigenerational tensions that result from the great political divide as well as tensions in the workplace, as more upper-age workers maintain positions well past traditional retirement ages.

Some of these tensions are manifesting themselves in a scorched-earth and win-at-all-costs fight, leaving many perplexed and unable to understand how we got to this point in our nation's history—and with little understanding as to where to go from here and how to heal the divide and resultant damage moving forward.

IMMIGRATION

Finally, we must recognize one the most complex and cumbersome issues of all, that of immigration. The United States, as well as many other regions of the world, struggles mightily with how best to find the appropriate balance of helping the world's most desperate while still protecting and maintaining the country's borders, security, and sovereignty. If this weren't complicated enough, the great political and cultural divide is front and center to the debate as well, with the far left staking positions completely at odds with the right and further demonizing and alienating its enemies in the process.

Neither party is serious about identifying long-term and sustainable solutions. Neither party is willing to take the

[74] "The History of Racism in America," *Smithsonian Magazine* (June 2020), https://www.smithsonianmag.com/history/158-resources-understanding-systemic-racism-america-180975029/.

necessary risks. Finally, neither party is seeing a political upside to potential solutions, leaving us all in the wake with a horrible drop-down menu of increasingly ghastly choices.

EXPONENTIAL TECHNOLOGICAL GROWTH

Much has been written, discussed, and even debated about the increasing role of technology in our daily lives. The ongoing debate about technology's benefits and challenges is almost irrelevant. There seems to be no prospect of slowing the relentless progression. Only in the realm of medical science, where ethicists have placed some constraints on the grounds of human and physiological ethics, has there been some moderation of science's potential and growth.

In the realm of business and society, there seem to be few limits on our hunger for convenience and speed in solving all of life's problems. This desire has led to the increasing advancement and utilization of robotics and artificial intelligence, calling into question many jobs and career pathways and risking the movement of large swaths of our contemporary workforce into the realm of potential obsolescence.

As recent events, such as global pandemics and other major health events, bring about miraculous advancements in medical science and practice, these realities will likely lead to further investments in vaccines, treatments, and therapies of all types, all at lightning speed and effectiveness. Could such movement and (seeming) power lead to an arrogance that humanity can cure all ills with science and technology, leading to perpetuating cycles and even potential avoidance of longer-term and more sustainable health objectives?

Finally, the advancement and integration of communication

technology into all aspects of our daily lives—with smartphones, smart houses, smart cars, etc.—has left us better connected than ever. Yet many feel lost and alone, disconnected from friends, family, and society at large.[75] Future advancements could further erase the line between technology and biology, integrating such tools increasingly into our physiological, social, and career structures moving forward.

GLOBALIZATION

Globalization has been discussed in this analysis previously. While events such as the 2020 pandemic, acts of terrorism, and even war will serve to curtail the growth of globalism, such challenges are unlikely to end its unrelenting momentum. There are simply too many compelling and historical reasons for humankind to increase its sphere of influence and experience.

Humanity will continue to explore the fruits of global economies, societies, and cultures. The seemingly major events, such as those evidenced in the past few decades, will serve as mere speed bumps in the immensity of human history and our ultimate global ambitions.

CLIMATE CHANGE

This is an obviously controversial and ongoing debate with (apparently) no end in sight. Therefore, my discussion of this key area will be limited and pointed. Whatever the reasons, it

---

[75] Janna Anderson and Lee Rainie, "Concerns about the Future of People's Well-Being," Pew Research Center, April 2018, https://www.pewresearch.org/internet/2018/04/17/concerns-about-the-future-of-peoples-well-being/.

seems evident that weather will play an increasingly dramatic role in the evolution of world and human events.

These increasingly powerful cycles will have an impact on substantial population dislocations and possibly even mass migration between geographic regions of the world. While we grapple with and argue about the causes, the events and resultant damage will continue to present themselves, paying no attention to our dramatic discourse, constant denials, and inaction.

Mother Nature will continue to wreak havoc and disruption on all in her path. While we will eventually come to terms with the readjustments needed, societies, economies, and cultures will have to make the long-term allowances needed, yielding to a new normal and much ambiguity along the way.

ECONOMIC CONVULSION AND DISRUPTION

Economic disruption will be ongoing and take several forms. We will discuss a few at this juncture, but this will be a sampling only. The actual number and manifestations exhibited will be numerous.

First, will be career-pathway instability via the effects of globalization, climate change, and technological advancement. Entire jobs, careers, and even industries could well be devastated or transformed significantly.[76] It is well known that the pandemic has threatened travel and entertainment as well as all of the jobs and careers associated. Technology and artificial intelligence are currently threatening entire industries, such as taxi drivers and truckers. It is estimated that the same forces

[76] Neil Irwin, "It's the End of the World Economy as We Know It," *New York Times* (April 2020), https://www.nytimes.com/2020/04/16/upshot/world-economy-restructuring-coronavirus.html.

could well threaten traditionally safe professional careers, such as within the medical and even legal professions.

Next, will we populate an increasingly crowded career landscape as multiple generations occupy an ever-competitive workforce? While baby boomers hang on longer and delay retirement, they will likely be holding jobs later into their careers and increasingly hindering career pathways for those coming up behind them.

These realities could increase both tensions and opportunities, but there is little doubt that they will create pressures and even eventual blowback from younger workers feeling the pinch of delayed promotions and lost opportunities.[77] There will be pressures on business and the general economy to absorb the larger workforce and provide enough jobs and prospects to establish an equilibrium in the general economic environment.

Political instability would not generally fall in the realm of economic disruption, but it could very well be one of the most significant threats moving forward. Political wrangling and a divisive mentality in both political parties often leaves businesses and entire industries in the wake of such dysfunction. Particularly with substantial changes in the federal political structures from one party to the other, there tend to be moves to radically change major programs (health care, environmental, climate, etc.). The opposite party often takes diametrically opposed positions on important issues impacting business as well as the general economy. This lurching back and forth can breed much economic and business uncertainty as well as disastrous gaps in regulations and guidance from federal agencies and

---

77 Shannon Gausepohl, "Tackling 4 Key Challenges of the Multigenerational Workforce," *Business News Daily* (January 2018), https://www.businessnewsdaily.com/6609-multigenerational-workforce-challenges.html.

bureaucrats. This can take place over months and even years, leaving businesses and entire industries to fend for themselves.

A glaring and dire area of concern is the overutilization of debt and leverage by both business and governmental entities.[78] Increasing amounts of leverage and overspending have led to monstrous problems, leading to events such as the 2008 economic and financial crisis, which brought entire countries (such as Iceland and Greece) to the brink of default.

Finally, we are now in the grips of one of the largest and most prolonged pandemics in history, which is currently affecting the entire global landscape, shutting down and impacting entire economies for over a year. While it would seem this would not be a regular threat and occurrence, it seems eerily possible that we might see instances such as this (or even just the perceived threat) result in large-scale disruptions in regional and national economies as well as supply chains in the coming decades.[79]

CONCLUSION

We began this chapter talking about a few of the reasons why such significant changes are now a part of our current and emerging landscapes. After such an analysis, it is evident that the determination and drive of humanity to grow and evolve becomes a determining factor and issue. It is my opinion that these ambitions will continue to grow and will not be limited considerably.

---

78 Kimberly Amadeo, "Why US Deficit Spending Is Out of Control—Why Government Leaders Continue to Deficit Spend," *The Balance* (February 2021), https://www.thebalance.com/deficit-spending-causes-why-it-s-out-of-control-3306289.

79 Victoria Gill, "Coronavirus: This Is Not the Last Pandemic," BBC News, June 2020, https://www.bbc.com/news/science-environment-52775386.

6 KEY TAKEAWAYS: WHAT IS BRINGING ABOUT THIS NEW AGE?

1. There is a toxic and highly divisive political environment taking hold nationally and globally.
2. Irreversible and fast-paced social and cultural change, driven by changing ethos and demographics are taking place at an ever increasing pace.
3. Exponential technological change, driven by science, robotics, and artificial intelligence are quickly changing the industrial and global landscape.
4. Globalization; while stunted somewhat in an era of pandemics, the allure is too great, and it will continue at a rapid pace.
5. Climate change will dominate and influence national debates, discussions and eventually legislation. There will continue to be disagreements between ideological forces on all sides. This will result in an ongoing political and regulatory tug of war.
6. Economic convulsion and disruption will result from these and many more influences. We could be trapped in age of hyper disruptive battles, in which there will be no ready answers and little hope of pragmatism or cooperation.

7

WHY ARE WE NOT LIKELY TO AVOID THE IMPACT?

Research Participant: I have lost three jobs in the past eight years. The situation has been about the same each time. The businesses seemed to be positioned well, doing well … then the economy and/or industry shifted dramatically … in one case the business was sold.

Went from 0 to 60 … Then all hell breaks loose. You thought you were in the catbird seat … now suddenly you are on the outside looking in!

Straub/Researcher: Can you describe how it makes you feel?

Research Participant: I wasn't the only one impacted in each of these downsizings. There were tens and even hundreds. But you start to doubt yourself. You feel like people are looking at you differently, potential employers for sure … but even friends and family.

> It … it's just demoralizing and devastating. Why can't I keep a damned job! I used to be able to … I didn't even worry about it … but now … It's very hard not to lose faith.
>
> ***Researcher Note:*** *I gave this individual my card and asked for a call and update. I wanted to know when things turned around and improved. Unfortunately, I never received that call.*

While I am optimistic that we will eventually learn and find solutions to our country's and the world's problems, there is clearly much work to do and a long way to go before this happens. In the intermediate term, I am not optimistic that we will have much success in containing the impact of many of the problems we have identified to this point.

As noted throughout this work, it seems evident that the convulsions we are experiencing are continuing to increase in intensity. Additionally, the cycle times seem to compress. As a result, there are eight reasons I believe we are destined for more of these movements, and they are as follows:

1. Due to the globalized nature of many of the problems we face, the complexity will be significant and prolonged. Additionally and unfortunately, we have much more work and heavy lifting to do before we can successfully tackle the big problems we currently face on a global scale. Despite the fact that it seemed we were making great strides after World War II in key areas, creating world institutions like the United Nations, World Health Organization, and International Monetary Fund (to name a few), it seems those gains are being threatened by nationalistic leaders, populist political

movements as well as the institutions corruption and ineptitude.

2. As noted earlier, mankind quite simply will not be contained. Every medical and scientific breakthrough provides ever more evidence and leads to this inevitable conclusion: there is no problem we can collectively create that we cannot solve. A recent publication highlighted a scientific discovery that new super-enzymes eat plastic bottles—not only eat them but consume them at ever-increasing rates.[80] This points to industrial-scale applications that might well solve the global recycling dilemma in regard to this widely used, popular, and necessary resource. This is obviously a discovery with immeasurable potential and should surely be celebrated. What is a bit disconcerting, however, is that these very types of solutions are what feed the somewhat dangerous delusion that there is no problem we cannot solve, no matter how great.
3. Many of the long-term solutions needed and necessary will be painful and unpopular. As is now the case, retiring (last-term) or retired congress people will talk wistfully and pragmatically about such solutions and why they are needed. However, there are few sitting politicians (with future ambitions) who will be so bold and possess the courage to propose the solutions needed.
4. We do not have political, social or economic systems that reward the type of long-term, pragmatic, and sustainable modeling or actions that will be

80 Damian Carrington, "New Super-Enzyme Eats Plastic Bottles Six Times Faster," *The Guardian* (September 2020), https://www.theguardian.com/environment/2020/sep/28/new-super-enzyme-eats-plastic-bottles-six-times-faster.

necessary to solve the world's problems. Therefore (and unfortunately), we will have to have no other choices left before we finally deal with the problems that need to be addressed. While it is certainly easy to judge, there will be an understandable reluctance to take the painful medicine that will be the ultimate required treatment. Those politicians and political parties brave (or insane) enough to propose and actually implement the solutions required will likely look like monsters to the general populace. It will take a great force of will to make the moves and stay the course in the face of much resistance, disinformation, and misdirection.

5. While in perpetual denial, we will be looking eagerly for charismatic, dynamic, and superhuman political saviors to rescue us from ourselves and such horrific realities. We can see evidence of these type of leaders on the landscape currently. It could be argued that Barack Obama and Donald Trump were different sides of the same coin in this respect. We will see the same thing on a global scale. This is evidenced by populist leaders beginning to emerge in different regions of the world.

   Hopefully, extremists will not rule the day as we edge closer to these oncoming challenges, landing us under the influence of the next Hitler, Stalin, or Mao. Research and understand the despair of the post-WWI years, and you will learn that hopeless and poverty-stricken environments were a fertile breeding ground for such leaders and tyrants. The risk is that while we are looking for false prophets and the convenient and apparently painless answers they promise, we will not be doing the tough and painful work it will take to solve our actual and ongoing problems.

6. The world's environmental and population issues will continue to multiply. According to recent speculation and projections from Jorgen Randers, the population will peak at 8.1 billion in the year 2040. However, as we are at 7.8 billion in 2020, this projection could seem somewhat optimistic.[81] Some scientists, however, see population topping out at over 10 billion people at some point post–2100.[82]

   These population levels will continue to tax our environment and ecosystems. The results of this overuse of resources can be realistically estimated. Many agree that it will pose threats and challenges and could result in changing social, cultural, and economic landscapes. The predictions are not all negative, however. Several scientists believe that world population is slowing and will top out just under 10 billion. Many also agree that the planet should be able to feed and supply resources for such populations, if managed wisely.[83]

---

81 Darrell Bricker and John Ibbitson, "What Goes Up: Are Predictions of a Population Crisis Wrong?" *The Guardian* (January 2019), https://www.theguardian.com/world/2019/jan/27/what-goes-up-population-crisis-wrong-fertility-rates-decline#:~:text=J%C3%B8rgen%20Randers%2C%20a%20Norwegian%20academic,2040%2C%20and%20then%20decline.%E2%80%9D.

82 Gail Tverberg, "Why I Don't Believe Randers' Limits to Growth Forecast to 2052," *Business Insider* (September 2013), https://www.businessinsider.com/why-i-dont-believe-randers-limits-to-growth-forecast-to-2052-2013-12.

83 Heinz-Wilhelm Strubenhoff, "Can 10 Billion People Live and Eat Well on the Planet? Yes," Brookings.edu, April 2015, https://

7. Current societies, cultures, and economies are bridging the gap toward the concept known as the *technological singularity*. This concept is defined as the "hypothetical point in time at which technological growth becomes uncontrollable and irreversible, resulting in unforeseeable changes to human civilization."[84] This trend and potential reality is evidenced in the recent and exponential growth in scientific inquiry, robotics, and artificial intelligence. Vast sectors of our economy will be under siege, with entire industries—such as transportation, management, and administration—in jeopardy. There could be mass displacement. Will the jobs in new and emerging sectors be enough to fill the gaps? And how many will be unable to adapt quickly enough and be left behind?
8. While somewhat of an offshoot of technology and environment, I feel the realm of biomedical issues—and more specifically, health crises and pandemics—should have its own place and identification. The global impact of the 2019 and 2020 pandemic seem to have in one swift move redefined society, the economy, and the global environment. Is it possible to hit the reset button, or will this world of masks, lockdowns, and fear be the new normal—a world always on edge, looking with paranoid and cautious eyes at the global environment we live in? This new reality stands in dramatic contrast

---

www.brookings.edu/blog/future-development/2015/04/28/can-10-billion-people-live-and-eat-well-on-the-planet-yes/.

84 Jayshree Pandya, "The Troubling Trajectory Of Technological Singularity," Forbes.com, February 2019, https://www.forbes.com/sites/cognitiveworld/2019/02/10/the-troubling-trajectory-of-technological-singularity/?sh=56afd5dd6711.

> to the irrepressible optimism that existed before this world-scale catastrophe presented itself.

As has been demonstrated throughout the course of human history, people are resilient, and we will no doubt learn and grow. In the face of the issues identified, can we grow sufficiently to keep pace with the monumental challenges we face? Can political and social structures evolve and change as needed to help lead humanity toward sustainable and equitable solutions? Can we muster the will and discipline to hold ourselves and our leaders accountable for the results needed in the coming decades?

As noted earlier, I have a long-term optimism that we will do this and more. In the interim, it will be a much trickier landscape. The question remains: will we find our will in the coming decades, or could it be centuries before we integrate the learning and discipline necessary to move sustainably forward? These are the overriding questions, and all of humanity's future will be at stake.

Next, we will examine what the specific challenges and opportunities of this new environment will be. There are many, and they must be understood.

6 KEY TAKEAWAYS: WHY ARE WE NOT LIKELY TO AVOID IMPACT?

1. Humankind will not be contained. We will not slow the pace of technological and scientific change.
2. Actual and long-term solutions will be painful and politically unpopular. It will be much easier for politicians to pander to donors and electorates than to make the tough decisions needed.
3. We do not yet have political, social, or economic systems that reward such pragmatic and courageous behaviors and actions by public and private representatives.
4. We will continue to be in a state of perpetual denial of our realities and challenges, instead looking for charismatic, dynamic and seemingly superhuman political saviors. We will continue to fall for a series of false prophets and snake-oil salesmen because we do not have the desire or courage to face the realities of our current predicament.
5. The world's problems will continue unabated, from population growth and immigration to climate change. Such issues are very complicated and evasive of the well-collaborated global solutions needed and required.
6. Exponential technological growth will continue to provide great opportunity but also incredible risks and threats. Threats include job loss via robotics and artificial intelligence, global health threats, as well as the ongoing challenges of climate change.

8

THE CHALLENGES AND OPPORTUNITIES OF THE NEW ENVIRONMENT

Straub/Researcher: You noted earlier that losing your job in 2009 was a net positive for you … can you describe what you mean?

Research Participant: Well, I was forty-eight years old, and the thought of going back on the treadmill, getting another job … just to be run through the ringer and jerked around again. That just didn't appeal to me.

Straub/Researcher: What did you do differently?

Research Participant: I always had this idea for a business/nonprofit … I decided this was the kick in the pants I needed, this was the right time to give it a try. So I did.

Straub/Researcher: Can you describe it to me?

Research Participant: I started a nonprofit that helps homeless individuals start businesses utilizing social entrepreneurship principles and micro-lending ... the goal is to help define an alternative pathway for them. It has been very rewarding and inspiring to see folks transform, to see their true potential.

Straub/Researcher: Is this a full-time venture for you currently?

Research Participant: It is an ongoing one ... After completing my doctorate, I pursued being a professor in higher education ... this worked out, and I now do that full time. But I still run my nonprofit on the side, and it is still a big part of my mission and life.

Throughout the course of our examination, we have highlighted the many trials we will likely face nationally and globally. Before we discuss the opportunities that will present themselves along the way, let's first look at a summary of the challenges of our approaching realities.

CHALLENGES OF THE NEW LANDSCAPE

GLOBALIZATION

You will note that globalization is viewed as both a challenge and an opportunity. While we will highlight certain opportunities, these structures and realities will continue to be a messy undertaking. With resultant issues like immigration, migration, and many cultural challenges, this issue will prove to be complicated and chaotic. it has the potential to divide regions, communities, and even families.

MARKET ACCESS

A very real and distinctive offshoot of the pandemic will be the issue of market access. Societies and economies took such access for granted previously but now no longer have such a guarantee. There have proven to be many winners and losers in the era of coronavirus. The lasting impact and extent of the gains and losses will be calculated and assessed in the coming years and decades. There is no doubt that we will reexamine jobs, careers, lifestyles, and ultimately fairness resultant on such analysis and the conclusions reached.

Based on these analyses will be the realization that some lives, occupations, and entire communities were deemed expendable, while others were not. This might well serve as a wedge. Even greater divides could emerge between segments of our population regionally, nationally, and globally.

COORDINATION AND EMERGENCY PLANNING

The inability of our regional and national political structures to come together—to take a cohesive and coordinated lead in guiding our nation through this period—was very much on display. Can the United States, in particular, muster the introspection to analyze what took place during this period, assessing how we might better prepare ourselves in the future for such cataclysmic circumstances? Based on preliminary signals and signs, the prospect does not seem encouraging. There is little sign that such movement and reflections are taking or will take place.

The ability of health care systems to learn from this experience and grow access to acceptable levels will be an ongoing challenge. The test will not only be the ability to adapt but also to provide access to specific and coordinated resources via local, state, and national governments. The corresponding challenge is our state and federal structures' inability to stay diligent and consistently focused on such important issues. There remains a demonstrated propensity to hit the reset button, moving quickly beyond and back to business as usual.

The aftermath of the pandemic will undoubtedly test the state and national social safety nets and support systems. Large populations will deal with housing and even food insecurity in the wake of this global pandemic. Will it be possible for agencies to keep pace with the significant needs in our country's intermediate future?

Market access will be scrutinized extensively as we build a new world order following the pandemic. Global systems and structures will be analyzed; business platforms will be redesigned with a look toward more balanced and accessible systems and structures.

Additionally, entire industries will be reexamined and their business models redefined, particularly those that were forced to shutter because of health, safety, and security concerns. Longtime staples of our cultural and entertainment landscape—movies, concerts, amusement parks, cruise ships, and air travel—will likely be reevaluated in regard to their overriding business structures, profit potential, and sustainability.

All of these challenges and issues will come full force and in unrelenting fashion, tasking leaders at all levels to find equitable ways to divide desperately needed and potentially scarce resources. With increasing urgency and relentless demands, no doubt many of these choices and decisions will seem arbitrary and unfair.

OPPORTUNITIES AND THE NEW LANDSCAPE

While there are no doubt daunting challenges, there are several opportunities that could emerge and provide a much more stable foundation moving forward. While the proposed and highlighted solutions will be complex, there will eventually need to be movement on each of these issues to provide a sustainable and continuous landscape for society, business, and the overall economy.

NATIONAL SPENDING CONSTRAINTS

First are needed constraints on governmental borrowing, tied especially to rational limits as a percentage of gross domestic product. While it is certainly understandable that national governments require flexibility to deal with major events—such as war, health crises, and environmental disasters—it is similarly evident that most governments (particularly the United States) never seem to find the right time or circumstances in which to reduce deficit spending as well as the resultant debt levels. We see a constant pattern: either the country is in too dire economic circumstances or the recovery is too fragile. There never seems to be the exact Goldilocks zone or conditions in which to make the necessary moves.[85]

Fiscal discipline must be required of governments, similar to balanced budget constraints, to force politicians to make difficult and ultimately unpopular choices. Unfortunately, for all the aspects our founders got correct with our Constitution,

---

[85] Kimberly Amadeo, "Will the US Ever Pay Off Its Debt? Why Our Debt Is So High and How We Can Fix It," Thebalance.com, February 2021, https://www.thebalance.com/will-the-u-s-debt-ever-be-paid-off-3970473.

they failed to provide such spending constraints, and present constitutional structures make it very difficult to enact them.

PRISON AND SENTENCING REFORM

Fortunately, this next proposed solution is moving forward currently. Our decades of "three strikes and you're out" and tough-on-crime policies has led to over-incarceration of certain subsets of our population, particularly minorities—severely damaging communities, trust in the government, and the stability of family units. Large segments of our society are condemned to poverty, underemployment, and a single-parent family structure that provides little strength or stability.[86]

There are currently moves toward abolishing mandatory sentences and incarceration for minor drug offenses, as well as a de-emphasis on privatized or for-profit prisons. More importantly, we must move toward what the framers of our Constitution had in mind: equal justice under the law and a legal system that is blind to race and social strata.

GLOBALIZATION

Collectively, we must find new frameworks and a more appropriate balance in respect to our globalized reality, understanding both the potential and the considerable risk. As was highlighted earlier, through the course of human history, we could not be contained or constrained from our grand and global ambitions. In this light, it will be important to continue

86 Wendy Sawyer and Peter Wagner, "Mass Incarceration: The Whole Pie 2020," Prinsonpolicy.org, March 2020, https://www.prisonpolicy.org/reports/pie2020.html.

to develop, manage, and support global institutions (such as the UN, WHO, and IMF) that work to further global growth, coordination, and balance.[87] While it is understandable that some are suspicious of such institutions and their motives, they remain the best and necessary hope to achieve the required equilibrium. Therefore, it seems practical to support these institutions while working diligently to reform their structures, provide accountability, and aggressively weed out corruptive players and practices.

As part of the global structure, all countries will need to work together to identify and work toward long-term and sustainable solutions to population migration issues that face many regions of the world. We are in essence a world of migrants and immigrants. We must acknowledge this and embrace the opportunities and challenges that come within this reality, while also balancing the realities of national guidelines and structures.

POLITICS

It will be incumbent on our nation (and others) to experiment with and identify alternative political structures in an attempt and with the goal of healing the great divides that have emerged. These divides are currently being exploited by political partisans, media, and moneyed interests, as well as those nefarious actors looking to stir division, strife, and chaos while sriving for geopolitical gain.

Why is this so crucial? As distasteful and challenging as

---

[87] NG Laura, "What Is the Main Role of International Institutions? Political, Financial, and Humanitarian Perspectives," grin.com, 2015, https://www.grin.com/document/337372.

politics are currently, these very structures are the mechanisms that will ultimately allow us to correct the problems that face us currently. So what might these new structures look like, and what might be the influences to bring solutions to the forefront? In some ways, not much different than those currently—just improved and tweaked a bit for performance and effectiveness.

In the United States, it seems as though releasing the stranglehold of the current two-party system might be a good start. This will not come without considerable fight and controversy. Our two dominant parties currently have the country and all of its trappings divided up very conveniently for their considerable benefit. A third party into which the substantial number of moderates on both sides could coalesce would seem to be a desirable outcome.

A reversal or reworking of Citizens United, the Supreme Court ruling that opened the political floodgates to corporate America and moneyed interests, will be needed. Currently, many local and state elections are masterfully impacted by large political action committees and other interest groups, which often have little to no connection to the locale being influenced. There primary interest is on the impact that seat or seats will have on the national balance of power between the major political parties.

Next, we will consider what (substantial) forces might be needed to bring about this new political structure. Moderates swing elections regularly and have to be considered in most election scenarios. How long will it be until they raise their voices and insist on a more influential seat at the political table?

Social media could be utilized to start such a movement, and utilizing this power and momentum could provide the push needed to sway elections in more worthwhile and pragmatic directions.[88] When the two primary parties overplay their hands and use and abuse the electorate to extremes, such movements could and should gain momentum and force the pendulum back toward the center.

Unfortunately, due to the terminal dysfunction in our federal political systems, it is likely that solutions will be slow. We may even have to hit the proverbial wall before enough force will be applied to bring about the needed changes. Hopefully, we will find the wisdom before irreparable damage is done to our national safety net and retirement system.[89]

DISRUPTION AND EXPONENTIAL CHANGE: THE NEW NORMAL

Ultimately, the lesson learned is that the current momentum and exponential change is not likely to be reversed. We may be able to slow it a bit to give our societies, cultures, and economies a bit more time to adapt. But eventually, these historic movements will take shape and reconfigure our national and even global landscape.

Therefore, it will be incumbent on all of us to get as high on the lookout as conceivable and look as far ahead as possible, in an effort to provide more lead time, allowing us to position and adapt to the approaching realities. This adaptation will need to occur on multiple levels, considering our individual, family, and career prospects simultaneously.

---

88 Athar Bhat, "Positive and Negative Effects of Social Media on Politics," Thriveglobal.com, April 2019, https://thriveglobal.com/stories/positive-and-negative-effects-of-social-media-on-politics/.

89 Sean Ross, "How Congress Retirement Pay Compares to the Overall Average," Investopedia.com, December 2020, https://www.investopedia.com/articles/markets/080416/how-congress-retirement-pay-compares-overall-average.asp.

6 KEY TAKEAWAYS: THE CHALLENGES AND OPPORTUNITIES OF THE NEW ENVIRONMENT

1. There is seemingly terminal dysfunction in state and federal governments.
2. There will likely be more convulsive environments ahead, leading to erratic social, cultural and business environments.
3. Prison sentencing reform will hopefully keep families together and provide more stability, particularly in minority communities.
4. National legislation should be enacted to require spending constraints as related to U.S. GDP.
5. New frameworks and structures should be established to manage and control immigration patterns and global health considerations.
6. A reimagining of our national political structure and discourse is called for, including open primaries, reduction in gerrymandered districts, and reformed political spending regulations.

THE THIRD CONVULSION:
INDUSTRY CONSOLIDATION AND "THE DEAL"

COMPONENTS OF 6E THINKING

- adaptability and toughness
- practicality
- strong and stable relationships
- scenario planning
- lifelong learning

When I joined the company in 1983, it was both by my desire and at my father's urging. I had not yet finished college, but he and my brother approached me about joining the business. While Ron's wife, Kathy, had joined the company and had the accounting and financial operations well under control, Wally and Ron felt that great opportunities and a major growth spurt lay ahead due to the recent addition of the agricultural dealership operations.

It was very exciting and rewarding for me to join the organization and work in the family business. It was also nice to be back in my hometown. I attacked both my role in the business and association with our community with enthusiasm.

After about five years, however, I found several things disconcerting to me as a next-generation member of the fledgling business. While I loved working for the business and with my family, I was starting to entertain reservations in regard to investing my future in the business—particularly in the industry in which our company resided.

There were several things that troubled me. First was the fact that in many ways, we did not control our own destiny. The manufacturer ultimately controlled the nature of the relationship via the manufacturer's agreement and terms of the contract. Dealers had defined rights under the contractual agreement; however, they were controlled by and skewed to the manufacturer's advantage.

Second, the nature of the relationship between manufacturers and dealer groups was and still is asymmetrical. Initially, the manufacturer sees dealer financials every month—not because we submit them, but because the manufacturer is able to retrieve them from our sanctioned and required dealer business information systems. They also control the terms of the contract, with nominal input and influence from dealers.

Third, there was and is a potentially coercive and controlling relationship between manufacturers and the dealers that represented them in the marketplace. This is not just an agriculture industry phenomenon; this happens in trucking, construction, and the automobile industry as well. But it definitely had an impact and effect early on in our business association and would be prevalent throughout our extended relations.

The manufacturers could and would at times put immense pressure on dealers to stock defined levels and targets of their equipment. Also, there was increasing pressure on reaching defined sales and market-share targets. While this was understandable to an extent, at times it could be unreasonable, manipulative, and even heavy-handed.

Fourth, the future indicators of the business and industry were for fewer major manufacturers of equipment and ever smaller numbers of (end user/farmer) customers. Both were irreversible and accelerating trends.

Finally, dealers such as our operation were being encouraged to buy more stores and increase our base and scale of operations. While this presented opportunities due to volume-based incentive structures (more sales equaled greater discounts, resulting in greater profits), this arrangement could change and be reordered by the manufacturer at any time. The initial structures that enticed dealers into larger organizations (stores as well as market structure) could be switched at virtually any time by the manufacturer.

These concerns became very disconcerting to me in my early thirties, and I discussed with my family the prospect of leaving the company. I found it very difficult to invest my future in such an unbalanced and potentially controlling, even manipulative business relationship. I had finished my bachelor's degree by that time and was partway through my first master's degree. My alternate pathway involved continuing on with my education, finishing the master's, and eventually completing a doctorate degree—this with the intent of transitioning my career into academia and possibly even management and business consulting.

While my father, brother Ron, and sister-in-law Kathy (our CFO) were initially very supportive of my concerns and potential changes, as time went on, my father became anxious about the future of the company without my continued involvement. It was at this point the family made me an offer: if I would agree to move forward with the company, they would agree to pay for any and all education I would want to pursue part-time as we moved forward with the company's development and future.

This proved acceptable and desirable to me. It would allow me to stay with the family business but simultaneously continue to grow my educational portfolio, allowing for more and different options should something happen to the company and its business relationships with our primary manufacturer. The family showed incredible integrity and met its obligation and promise at every turn. Through my continued involvement with the company, I was able to earn two master's degrees and a doctorate over the span of twenty years.

It seemed that everyone agreed it was a mutually beneficial proposition. Via the advanced training I had access to and received, the company was able to grow substantially while achieving increased levels of management sophistication. This family and organizational growth would allow the company to become a well-respected leader in our community, region, and industry.

This period of growth would eventually lead to our company being one of the largest dealer networks in North America. But most importantly, it would result in our work and engagement together as a family over the next few decades, in the business we treasured as well as in the community we loved.

PART THREE

THE PROMETHEAN FRAMEWORK: HOW TO POSITION FOR SUSTAINABILITY AND SUCCESS IN CONVULSIVE ENVIRONMENTS

The demigod Prometheus was famous in Greek mythology for being a trickster and an enthusiast of mankind, believing in their abilities, aspirations and desires. He was also known to be boldly creative, even defiantly original in his behaviors and actions.

Prometheus was so attuned to humankind that he was guilty of human like flaws in the form of overreach and an outsized ambition. These negative qualities gained him the attention and scorn of the God Zeus who had him banished and chained to a rock on an abandoned island to suffer unimaginable tortures.—***Encyclopedia Britannica***

9

MY RESEARCH JOURNEY AND THE PROMETHEAN FRAMEWORK

Straub/Researcher: You lost your job in your mid- to late forties … what were your thoughts and feelings at that time?

Research Participant: I would be lying if I didn't say I was a bit scared … not a great time in your life to lose a job. Especially one I had for over twenty years.

Straub/Researcher: What were the circumstances in regard to losing your job?

Research Participant: I had worked for a gentleman and his wife in a business. It was a great job and situation. He and his wife had long discussed with me their desire for me to take over the business when they got to retirement. The timing was right, and it seemed like a great opportunity.

But then life happened … His wife died of cancer about ten years ago. He got remarried, and that is when things changed.

Straub/Researcher: How so?

Research Participant: His previous wife just did the books and did not want to be very involved in the business … his new wife was a 180-degree difference. She was into everything.

I had been the general manager and pretty much had free rein as long as I managed within budgets and the business remained profitable (that had always been the case). Now I had to work through the new wife. She was my "partner" now. It was not a great deal.

She also informed me that I was going to buy them out at "fair market" if I was going to ever assume ownership of the business … I didn't think that was going to go well … so I decided to push the envelope with the owner … I lost.

Straub/Researcher: So you left the business?

Research Participant: More like … got escorted to the door. [Chuckle]

Straub/Researcher: What were your plans after that?

Research Participant: I actually looked at it as an opportunity … my wife and I planned to move to Florida. I had some opportunities (and family) there that I wanted to pursue and we wanted to get closer to.

Straub / Researcher: What changed? That obviously did not happen.

Research Participant: Your brother Ron happened. It was so weird … I had known him casually through the years … but he would have been one of the last people I would have expected to give a crap if I lost my job. But there he was.

Straub/Researcher: Why was that?

Research Participant: Initially, it was because of him and a few other folks that did not want to see me leave town … they liked having me around I guess.

Then it morphed … your brother mentioned that your firm was needing a GM for your Great Bend store. He asked if I wanted to drop by and take a look … The rest is history … I loved the opportunity and the people. It has been a great fit, and I hope to retire here.

Straub/Researcher: Anything else to add?

Research Participant: Just the importance of a strong network. There were some people that really stepped up and took an interest in me and my situation. And as I noted, some I would never have predicted, like your brother. It was very cool …

Researcher Note: *He did retire after fifteen successful years with our company—about two years before the sale of our business.*

ABOUT THE RESEARCH

The goal of my research was to identify frameworks, practices, and strategies that helped individuals survive and even prosper in the wake of the 2008 US and global economic collapse. I did both qualitative and quantitative research studies to gain a rich three-dimensional view of the phenomenon—it served as one of the first research studies completed with five years of data. In the qualitative study, I interviewed forty-two participants, most of whom had lost employment and had to go through the process of regaining work as a result. I also interviewed a select number of employers and placement professionals to look at such issues from their perspective.

The quantitative study surveyed 490 participants with a specially designed research instrument to isolate factors and practices that made the most difference in outcomes (success or failure) in the job-searching process. My three-year study yielded a significant catalogue of helpful knowledge pointing to the importance of relational networks, adaptability, physical vibrancy, and the importance of managing one's career and risk profile. I further isolated a measurement tool that should prove helpful in determining how well people are situated to ride out future convulsive economic cycles.

BUILDING A BETTER BOAT

Imagine yourself in a boat on open waters—waters that have suddenly turned threatening and treacherous due to an unforeseen storm. Within the course of hours, you have gone from a calm, relaxing day to being tossed mercilessly, with the threat of capsizing at any moment. Suddenly, your very survival depends on the tools you have on the boat as well as the stability of the boat itself.

This seems a fitting metaphor for what the past decade (or so) must have felt like for many in the American workforce, the treacherous waters in this case being the general economy and the boat being individuals who must navigate those dangerous and unpredictable conditions.

Severe macroeconomic disruption is quickly becoming a looming global, national, and even local crisis. The impact of convulsive economic cycles is responsible for large-scale disorder in many lives, businesses, industries, and economies. These disruptions result in fiscal instability as well as erratic and irregular employment conditions. Many of those displaced in the past decade have struggled to reengage and reconstruct their part of the economic landscape.

David Walker, former US comptroller general of the currency and a loud proponent for sustained and structural change, likens our current situation to that of the Roman Empire in decline. Describing the foundation of the US government as a burning platform of unsustainable practices and policies, leading to expensive over commitments and ever-increasing deficits,[90] he goes on to note that the United States is not exempt from a debt crisis (despite the ability to print via our benchmark currency), adding that we have economic risks that can ultimately result in serious inflationary pressures. Mr. Walker believes strongly that the repercussions could be sudden, convulsive, and very painful for extended periods of time.

---

[90] Jeremy Grant, "Learn from the Fall of Rome, US Warned," *Financial Times* (August 2007), https://www.ft.com/content/80fa0a2c-49ef-11dc-9ffe-0000779fd2ac.

As the global environment continues to become more erratic and governments exist in a state of perpetual denial, there will be more economic and actual resources devoted to fighting the fires that will develop. Some researchers predict that almost 17 percent of the workforce will be composed of older adults moving forward, up from 13 percent in 2000. Painting an even more graphic picture, the older labor force is expected to increase at a rate more than five times faster than the overall labor population. More seniors will be putting off retirement. With almost 70 percent of fifty- to seventy-year-olds expecting to work past traditional retirement age or never retire at all, employment is becoming a necessity rather than an option for the seasoned worker.[91]

The debt crisis is a worldwide phenomenon, with developing nations leading the charge; according to the Economist World Debt Clock, global public debt has soared in the past ten years to over $258 trillion.[92] There is seemingly no end in sight to the world's outsized appetite for unsustainable living standards. Developing nations are now clamoring for goods and lifestyles unimaginable only a few decades ago.

I predict that the results of this untenable economic course as well as continued growth of populations throughout the world will lead to unprecedented and unanticipated challenges.[93]

---

[91] Bill Jean Miller and Steve Nyce, "Which Workers Are Delaying Retirement and Why?" *Towers Watson Insider* (September 2014), https://www.nasra.org/files/Topical%20Reports/Plan%20Design/Towers-Insider-Which%20Employees%20Are%20Delaying%20Retirement%20and%20Why.pdf.

[92] "The Global Debt Clock," *The Economist*, https://www.economist.com/content/global_debt_clock.

[93] "Population," UN.org, https://www.un.org/en/sections/issues-depth/population/.

Economic spasms will become more pronounced and exhibit ever shorter cycles, resulting in a US and global situation bordering on the disastrous.

I now propose a new paradigm: the Promethean Framework. We now captain a larger and stronger vessel, with sophisticated scanning and environmental monitoring equipment comprised of leading-edge components for surviving the biggest storms imaginable. Imagine a new type of vessel that allows you to stay upright and above water in the worst conditions. You will use the energy and force of the tumultuous environment to actually propel you forward, flourishing and growing both personally and professionally. In short, we propose building and navigating a new type of boat, one specially designed and built to routinely navigate such dramatic and convulsive environments.

So how should we position ourselves in the decades to come? My proposed framework will help you learn and adopt a fresh set of strategies and practices that will better allow you to navigate such potentially treacherous environments.

Defining and learning this framework and the skills associated are within reach for each of us, but we must first come to terms with and acknowledge the potential issues and realities at hand—understanding first and foremost that such a mindset will be necessary, even crucial, to ensuring our long-term personal and economic well-being. We will refer to the skills needed to build this stronger, more solid boat—and outfit it with anchors that will allow it to remain upright no matter the conditions—as the *Promethean Framework.*

THE PROMETHEAN FRAMEWORK

The name of my doctoral studies and resultant framework is inspired by the Greek god Prometheus. Prometheus was chained to a rock in a remote location as punishment for his bad and rebellious choices.[94] Ironically, Prometheus has become a mythical figure representing such current and relevant traits as human striving, as well as the risk of overreaching and unintended consequences. Much like Prometheus, present-day society is chained to a rock of our own making, evidenced by debt-laden countries, governmental-system breakdowns, and periods of intense economic instability. These issues have many stuck between a metaphorical rock and a hard place.

However, Prometheus was also acknowledged for his faith in human abilities to understand and manage complexities. Like Prometheus, we can break the chains from our rock and move purposefully toward a new, more sustainable future. My studies uncovered much reason for optimism, particularly the resiliency of the human spirit.

Throughout my qualitative research, I saw examples of individuals who could have easily quit and become dependent on friends, family, and social safety nets. However, they pushed ahead and persevered—some in almost heroic ways, taking on second and in some cases third jobs to make ends meet. Furthermore, they did it in a rather undramatic fashion, making short-term sacrifices for their family's long-term needs and interests. Many of those interviewed ultimately feel that they gained much more than they lost through the process,

---

[94] Mark Cartwright, "Prometheus," *Ancient History Encyclopedia* (April 2013), https://www.ancient.eu/Prometheus/.

including a new perspective and understanding of what is truly important in life.

The Promethean Framework provides you with the tools to construct your new vessel, one built to face possible irregular conditions on open waters. What are all the requirements for the building of such a boat? What will help it to stay afloat? Do we have the skills and ability to bring it all together?

THE STRUCTURE OF THE FRAMEWORK

To start, visualize your boat as you, your family, and your direct environment—those things that you have the most impact and control over, including adaptability (locus of control), lifelong learning, flexible career timelines, and physical vibrancy. These are what are referred to as the *mental disciplines*. It is noteworthy that physical vibrancy is included in this grouping. The mental toughness, determination, and discipline required to stay constant in the pursuit of such physical vibrancy goals and routines is the reason it is included it in this particular category.

APPLICATION OF THE FRAMEWORK

It is important to make note of a few key facts in relation to applying this framework to your life and career. First, the earlier the better. While this research started out focused on those over fifty, as it progressed, it eventually focused on all working individuals. Obviously, younger individuals have more time to develop and implement the disciplines, structures, and practices identified.

Next, this framework should be viewed as a model. Each of the nine components integrates to form a successful life model. It is not recommended to pick and choose individual components; however, improving outcomes in any one of the nine should provide noticeable benefits. It would be expected that each individual will be stronger in certain areas and weaker in others; however, each component of the model should provide opportunities for enhancement at most stages of an individual's life.

Also, this model should prove malleable and adaptable for whatever times present themselves. All nine of the components of this model have been considered recognizable attributes for decades, even centuries, and we anticipate they will serve as a solid foundation for lives and careers moving forward well into the future.

Finally, this is not meant to be an end-all, fix-all for the human experience. There will be no such tool, especially in the historic and convulsive times that could be our new reality in coming decades. There will be no guarantees. There may be times in all of our lives when we will face substantial challenges. However the nine components of the Promethean Framework may help buffer (act as a shock absorber for) the effect of what eventually impacts our lives. Additionally, the three most important factors in the Promethean Framework—adaptability, physical vibrancy, and relational networks—should provide the ultimate reset button for rebooting lives and careers.

6 KEY TAKEAWAYS: THE PROMETHEAN FRAMEWORK

1. *Promethean Framework*—the framework that emerged from my four-year doctoral-dissertation research journey.
2. *Build a new boat*—a strategy highlighted by the Promethean Framework to navigate the treacherous waters of our new convulsive environments.
3. *Economic post-traumatic stress (EPTS)*—a unique form of stress associated with job and career disruption, evidenced by long-term unemployment, work-family separation, financial distress, family-unit instability, and severe loss of self-esteem and ability to function personally and economically.
4. *Work family*—the relationships and relational networks that often emerge in normal career/work environments, at times nearing the intensity of family bonds. These bonds are oftentimes suddenly, violently, and irreparably severed with little or no notice via job loss and career displacement.
5. *Lifetime earnings maximization*—the process of taking care of long-term income and career prospects, at times and possibly at the expense of maximizing short-term gains.
6. *Convulsive economic quotient*—as measured by the Promethean Measurement Tool, this distinct composite figure measures your unique ability to survive and prosper in pronounced convulsive economic cycles.

10

WHAT'S YOUR CONVULSIVE ECONOMIC QUOTIENT? AND WHY DOES IT MATTER?

Researcher Note: *My last qualitative participant happened quite by accident. I was on my way to a doctoral residency at Case Western Reserve when I picked up a conversation with this gentleman at Chicago O'Hare. He was also on a layover, and luckily we both had a couple hours to spare. I mentioned my research and the topic, and he was very interested to learn more and contribute his own (very incredible) story to the study.*

Straub/Researcher: Thanks for agreeing to an interview … While I was telling you a bit about my research journey and topic … you mentioned that you had a story you thought might be of interest. Tell me about your journey.

Research Participant: I worked in New York in the World Trade Center. This was [about] two years before 9/11. Now I work in Chicago. It is macabre to say and even think …

but had I still been working for my previous employer, I would likely have died. I lost friends and past coworkers that day …

Straub/Researcher: What were the circumstances of your job loss?

Research Participant: The firm I worked for was about fifty years old and had been very stable and well respected. But as the years went by and a new generation came into the mix … it kind of started to go south. You could see it, and you could feel it.

Straub/Researcher: How did that impact you and your plans?

Research Participant: It became evident to me and others that this was not going to end well. So I used the company's tuition assistance program to complete an MBA. I was able to do an accelerated course through a top school on the East Coast.

While my friends would be out partying or hanging out, I was completing this degree and working on other financial certifications. It was very intense and a lot of work.

Straub/Researcher: Did it pay off? Were you glad you did it?

Research Participant: Absolutely. The firm survived … but it had to downsize a couple of times to keep it all together. I got caught on the second one. I got a decent severance package and a fresh opportunity to reinvent myself.

Straub/Researcher: What form did that take?

> **Research Participant:** I am a certified financial planner and have my own business now. I feel so much more in control of my life, and I love helping people to get (and keep) their lives on track [financially].
>
> **Straub/Researcher:** Any regrets?
>
> **Research Participant:** Just the unease of what could have been on 9/11 … It really wracked the firm that I used to work for. They lost about 20 percent of the people to that tragedy. One of the owners perished.
>
> But … I am glad I got the professional experience in New York City. It definitely gives me a lot of credibility in the sector I work in currently.

As noted previously, the *convulsive economic quotient* (CEQ) is a term introduced in the studies and doctoral dissertation I completed in 2014.[95] The CEQ measures the nine key factors that contribute to an individual's sustainability in more erratic and convulsive social, cultural, and economic environments. An individual's CEQ is measured by the Promethean Framework Measurement Instrument (Appendix A) and is the composite figure that measures one's ability to survive and prosper in pronounced convulsive economic cycles.

This tool can also be utilized to assess individuals' relative status and positioning as they proceed through the different stages of life and career development. Adjustments can and should be made regularly, particularly at key ages and junctures of development. Therefore, in this stage of the book, I will

---

95 Larry Straub, "Promethean Framework and Measurement Instrument: Career Development, Maintenance, and Transitions in Convulsive Economic Cycles," Doctoral Dissertation, May 2014.

examine who the tool is best suited for as well as when and what type of modifications might be made at key points in an individual's progress.

WHAT'S YOUR CEQ?

Utilizing the Promethean Framework Measurement Instrument will determine not only your overall CEQ score but also the key subcomponents that make up the total score. The tool will show how you are positioned comprehensively as well as highlight specific areas that might be deficient and in need of special attention.

It is possible that individuals could have an overall satisfactory score but determine they have warning signs on the horizon in specific subcategories (such as disruption in significant relational groups). Additionally, the score could have been positive in the past but changes in the larger environment (possibly beyond your control) have shifted your relative positioning in key areas and clouded select parts of your outlook.

WHO IS THE CEQ IMPORTANT TO?

When the initial study was conducted, it was suggested and theorized that the target group was individuals in the early and middle stages of their careers. However, since that time, I have concluded that the target should be more encompassing. The Promethean Framework Measurement Instrument is constructed in a way that allows it to be utilized by individuals in many stages of life and career development. Perhaps it could be utilized with high school students as an educational and training instrument, assisting in giving a long-term view of how to position their lives and careers.

Undoubtedly, it should be utilized by college-age individuals and young/early-career adults. It will provide a forward look, allowing individuals more information in relation to how to best position their academic and early professional opportunities. This will hopefully lead to better informed choices in regard to education and occupations moving forward. It might also bring with it the realization that more convulsive environments might lie ahead and facilitate adopting the frameworks of adaptability and pragmatism.

Next would be midcareer adults—those with a decade or two of experience whose options for physical and career movement are still relatively fluid. By analyzing factors such as those outlined in the Promethean Framework, individuals can key on certain aspects of their life and career development, analyzing current and future employment realities, possibilities, and options for movement and growth. Such moves made by midcareer should provide time to learn new skills, even adapt to new industries while still optimizing career pathways and potential. Understanding these realities provides not only representative targets but also realistic timelines for career milestones and markers.

Finally, these models and the CEQ can be vitally important to late-career individuals—those who understand the importance of staying engaged with careers longer and more enthusiastically than once planned.[96] These individuals can realize and understand the importance of managing the long game while taking care of their lifetime earnings maximization.

---

[96] Jennifer Tomlinson, Marian Baird, Peter Berg, and Rae Cooper, "Flexible Careers Across the Life Course: Advancing Theory, Research, and Practice," *Sage Journals* (November 2017), https://journals.sagepub.com/doi/10.1177/0018726717733313.

WHY THE CEQ MATTERS

If, as I anticipate, we are going to find ourselves collectively immersed in more convulsive social, cultural, and economic environments, it seems reasonable to have our lives, our careers, and our families well positioned to weather such storms. Such environments can be dealt with sustainably, even successfully, if we design and position our lives and careers to serve as vehicles to see us through such challenging circumstances.

Further, in such irregular environments, it seems possible that there will be winners and losers, possibly even lost sectors of the economy and, at worst, lost generations. While it seems evident that the larger economies and societies are resilient over decades and centuries, individuals and smaller subsets of the populace many times are not.[97] It is for this reason that we must be vigilant in positioning our careers and earning potential for as many potential scenarios as possible.

WHAT IF ADJUSTMENTS ARE NEEDED?

As noted in the discussion of the Promethean Framework, and as evidenced by the Promethean Framework Measurement Instrument, each of the nine factors are isolated, measured, scored, analyzed, and can be constructively and proactively managed. Each factor that needs improvement can be assessed to determine the best course of action to shore up weaknesses and deal with concerns. For example, many individuals have

[97] Jan Bellens and George Atalla, "Will the Road to Recovery Lead to an Economy That's Revived or Reimagined?" EY.com, June 2020, https://www.ey.com/en_gl/covid-19/how-do-we-revive-the-economy-and-reframe-the-future.

not devoted the time or resources to build solid personal and career networks. This can be easily improved, while others may need to attack individual or family finances.

Each of these areas can be targeted and plans for improvement generated. Examples of strategies that could be implemented are changing jobs or industries; pushing back retirement plans or considering post-retirement income possibilities; changing careers; and even changing health and wellness patterns.

LIFETIME EARNINGS MAXIMIZATION

The definition of *lifetime earnings maximization* is the willingness and ability to adopt a financial framework that maximizes long-term earnings potential, sometimes even knowingly at the expense of short-term gains. This might include career moves that are lateral or even demotions to gain new opportunities, networks, or skill sets. It might involve repositioning to an altered career pathway later in your career, thereby allowing for a longer work landscape (for example, a less physically or mentally demanding job).

All this comes while balancing the sustainability of your career and income streams as well as individual goals and ambition. You must understand the importance of how you're positioned for late-career realities and retirement needs. And finally, you will acknowledge that the ultimate limits of your ability to earn can and will likely be tied to health and well-being, thereby prioritizing the care and maintenance of your physical and mental health.

6 KEY TAKEAWAYS: WHAT'S YOUR CEQ AND WHY DOES IT MATTER?

1. The *convulsive economic quotient* is the summary measure of the nine component tools of the Promethean Framework Measurement Instrument.
2. The CEQ measures individuals' positioning to be able to weather convulsive environments in regard to their lives and careers.
3. The tool is important to those in the early and middle stages of their career—those particularly with the time and career timelines available to make significant adjustments.
4. Each component of the framework is isolated and measured based on the analysis. Each can be impacted and improved as needed.
5. As we anticipate more convulsive environments moving forward, this type of analysis and strategy could prove crucial for sustainability in the coming decades.
6. *Lifetime earnings maximization* is the term that highlights the importance of long-term earning potential and realization, as opposed to the shorter-term-specific strategies normally employed.

THE FOURTH CONVULSION: RAPID GROWTH, THE NEXT GENS, AND "RIDING THE DRAGON"

COMPONENTS OF 6E THINKING

- positivity
- life and career management
- lifelong learning
- strong and stable relationships
- financial management

The next convulsion came in the form of what I refer to as *riding the dragon*. In this period of less than a decade, we would take our business to its greatest heights and eventually steer it away from its utmost threats and potential devastation.

During the decade of the 2010s, we would see our fortunes rise dramatically. This might seem wonderful; however, in a capital-intensive and traditionally highly leveraged industry, substantially increased levels of sales growth can result in perilous levels of risk due to the corresponding and increased debt levels required to keep pace. This was the case for our company and family.

Admittedly, the six years the business was growing to historical levels were certainly very heady and invigorating. However, there were ominous clouds on the horizon at every turn. Not only were we concerned about the business during these boom times, but we were also concerned about the family's prospects when the eventual downturn presented itself. How would not only the principle owners but our next-generation family members—managers and employees—be able to weather the anticipated decline?

About this time, we were looking to bring on another family member, one who had specialized financial talents that the business greatly needed. Would this be a good strategic decision for him and his family, and were the risks manageable? These were issues and decisions they would grapple with as they considered their options moving forward.

After much thought and reflection, it was decided to move forward and recruit our next family member, David, who would join Kristy and Darren as members of our next-generation team. Although the company was still at the peak of our business levels at the time (in excess of $110 million with 140 employees), even at this juncture, we saw warning signs on the horizon.

David and his wife felt the risks were worth it and that he was in a good time in his life to weather such uncertainty. He fit well with the organization and our current next-generation team; all were close personally and had strategically well-placed positions within the organizational structure. David's expertise as a CPA and Kristy's specialized training with her recent MBA would be welcome and valuable skills as the company moved forward.

There were two potentially lethal decisions that the manufacturer made during the early 2010s that dramatically changed the industry configuration and stacked the deck against dealers in our range of sales, scale, and market positioning. First, it moved its traditional volume bonus program away from total dollar volume of equipment sales. This was crucial for us. We had based many of our decisions on becoming a multistore dealership and operation on this particular structure and business model. It was working very well for us and many other dealers; with this model and structure,, we were able to enjoy a profitable and sustainable future.

The manufacturer moved away from rewarding total volume of sales and toward industry market-share attainment. This evolution changed the total dynamics of the industry, making it much more dominant for dealers to achieve aggressive market-share targets; making growth in sales all-important; and driving up the pressure to sell more and leverage the business even further via increased levels of debt.

Additionally, the manufacturer became increasingly forceful in requiring dealers to attain certain stocking and ordering requirements. In essence, at times it seemed they had hijacked our big-equipment inventory-procurement process, requiring increasing stocking levels and even pressuring orders of distressed big-equipment inventories.

While the motivations of the manufacturer could be understood, even justified in light of its own needs and market realities, that did not change the fact that the incentives that had enticed us into multistore ownership had been dramatically and most likely forever altered. While we enjoyed a good amount of success in achieving market-share targets for the company, it came via reduced profit margins and leveraging our company to levels that were increasingly worrisome and disconcerting.

The alternative, which seemed perilous, was to play the game as we had previously, seeing our profitability cut dramatically thanks to decreased volume bonuses and incurring the wrath of the manufacturer for lack of market-share attainment.

It was during this period that I and the family spent much time looking at different scenarios, weighing risks, and trying to predict likely outcomes. Being in my early fifties at this point in my life and career, it was very distressing to me to imagine finding myself out of a company and job in my mid to late fifties.

It was at this point that I decided to take the plunge and begin my doctoral journey at Case Western Reserve University. This four-year experience started the research that would eventually lead to the writing of this book. Further, it would provide me with new enlightenment and additional potential pathways should I need them down the road.

The family and company supported my journey throughout, honoring their commitment to allow me to pursue and assist me in achieving the educational goals necessary to grow intellectually and gain additional opportunities. Soon, these personal and professional moves would pay dividends, as a convulsive and somewhat frightening journey was about to begin. Could the family, next-generation members, employees, and other key stakeholders remain stable and sustainable through this dramatic and treacherous process and period?

PART FOUR

WELCOME TO 6E THINKING

For every complex problem, there's a solution that is simple, neat, and wrong.—***H. L. Mencken***
I like to say it's an attitude of not just thinking outside the box, but not even seeing the box.—***Safra A. Catz***

What an incredible journey we have taken together. Our voyage has allowed us to examine our historical, cultural, and economic roots as well as the traditions that bind us and define who we are—while, most importantly, examining the predictors with regard to what pathways we are likely to navigate moving forward. Before examining potential solutions to our complicated problems, it is first important to define and examine some of the constraints that lie before us. So let us first acknowledge a few realities that must be factored into adaptive strategies moving forward.

GLOBALIZATION CANNOT AND WILL NOT RECEDE

Even with the challenges globalization presents—and they are substantial—humanity will not be constrained. As we looked at historical migration and immigration patterns, we saw a consistent pattern of exploration and discovery, with populations constantly looking for new opportunities and improved lives. So despite challenges such as pandemics, terrorism, and threats from nefarious sources of every form and stripe, we will continue to see the glass as half full. No matter how bad it gets, there are still too many opportunities as well as prospective riches to be gained in a global economy.

Despite this acknowledgement, it is a reality that these global pursuits will always be complicated, risky, and controversial. It takes a simple and cursory examination of history to see that many of the issues we face today are born out of bitter and longstanding disputes that have existed for centuries between peoples and countries. It is necessary to acknowledge and understand that finding a global balance will be complicated and elusive but always worth the work and time it will take.

It must also be acknowledged that much of globalization will be centered on providing development opportunities to countries and their populations across the world. The last part of the twentieth and early parts of the twenty-first century are providing opportunities in regions of the world long relegated to the economic sidelines. For there to be long-term peace and stability, those progressions must be backfilled and expanded upon.

TECHNOLOGICAL GROWTH WILL NOT SLOW DOWN

The rate of technological growth is positioned to speed up, not slow down. From this point on, managing that growth and the challenges they present will seem akin to getting a drink of water out of a firehose. Despite the countless difficulties that result from technological growth, it also presents wondrous opportunities and potential solutions. And it's these opportunities that will keep us pushing forward nationally and globally, as regions and countries compete to stay positioned economically and culturally.

CAREERS, WORK, AND RETIREMENT

As highlighted, the nature of work and careers may well be changed forever. With increased convulsiveness likely the new normal, people will have a changed relationship with their work and career landscape. As disruptions to regular employment become commonplace, they will serve as a reminder that traditional career pathways as well as retirement plans may be more challenging to predict and navigate.

A more flexible pathway may be required in which individuals change and evolve career tracks, goals, and plans in a more fluid and malleable way. The divergence of opportunities between essential and nonessential, paid versus nonpaid, and professional versus nonprofessional economic participants (via the 2020 pandemic) will cause people to reconsider and reevaluate job, career, and even industry selection. This will take place on many levels and impact business in more ways than we can imagine or predict.

EQUALITY AND JUSTICE

It seems obvious that if you ask a thousand different people what equality and justice look like, you will get a thousand different perspectives. It is also apparent that thanks to massive social and cultural movements (such as #me-too and Black Lives Matter), there will be increasingly significant and complicated discussions concerning this very topic in America and other societies. While I am sure many would agree that such considerations are long overdue, there can be little doubt that the foundations of capitalism, political configurations, and even our legal structures will be questioned and challenged on many levels.

What is the definition of equality in a capitalist and free market system? Is it possible or even desirable? How do we package such ideologies and practices, protecting and teaching them in a manner that is understandable and palatable to newer generations? And finally, can we ever adequately arrive at such consensus and define what equality represents in our current and more polarized environments? We are seeing the initial stages of a raging societal, cultural, and political debate. It is passionate, ideological, and dogmatic, and seems positioned to dominate much of our landscape for the foreseeable future.

THE SOCIETAL SCHISM

There is a defined schism happening in our culture and society presently between those who believe opportunity and benefits must be earned and those who feel they should be a right (even an obligation); those who believe in the rule of law and those who believe it needs reimagined; and those who believe in science and institutional structures and those who do not, even bordering on actual distrust. This tear in our society and culture is being amplified and exploited by media companies, political parties, and moneyed interests hoping such movements and chaos will benefit them financially as well as structurally.

Interestingly, belief in the American Dream may well be the most impactful casualty of this current polarization and contempt. Many theorize we are about to experience the first generation that may, and likely will, be worse off than the previous generation. Some believe that the age of American exceptionalism is in the past and feel that what lies ahead will be far less prosperous and increasingly challenging.

POTENTIAL (MACRO) SOLUTIONS

First, a disclaimer: Since I have little power to get the recommendations that follow to become reality, this next segment should serve simply as a visioning exercise for a better, more sustainable tomorrow. The real work and heavy lifting will fall to economists, politicians, executives, and top-level academicians to devise potential solutions and workable models. As the Promethean model I propose is not overly complicated, the recommendations that follow are similarly straightforward—the concepts, that is. The execution and implementation are another issue altogether.

It must be acknowledged that in America, we like our solutions simple, effective, and quick. However, *simple* and *quick* likely won't fix what ails us. It wasn't simple and quick to get to where we are currently. The problems that are manifesting in our current reality have been created over decades, even centuries and could well take as long to identify and execute workable solutions.

While it must be recognized that there are no easy resolutions, I will venture to frame and envision the types of solutions needed moving forward. Additionally, I will examine the types of opportunities that might present themselves and provide potential solutions in the areas of politics, economics, society, and culture, as well as in the global arena.

POLITICAL

Any realistic solutions must include a dramatic softening of the grip of big money along with the major parties on our political and legislative landscape. This could be accomplished with tools such as the utilization of open primary systems that might deescalate the movement to the far extremes by both political parties. Also, reducing (or if possible, eliminating) the gerrymandering of congressional representation districts, which has made many elections a guaranteed (or at least safe) outcome for either of the two major parties, would be advisable.

There must be significant work on campaign finance reform, with the goal to reduce the influence of big money on politics. This will no doubt be complicated by rulings such as the 2010 Citizens United, but it must be a goal to ensure the concept of local control and truly representative governmental structures.

Additionally, we must stop the politicization of immigration reform and work to find sustainable long-term solutions. Hopefully, Republicans in particular will read the tea leaves, accept the coming demographic and cultural changes, and position their party and structures for a more realistic and sustainable future.

There must also be forms of legitimate and binding constraints on federal and deficit spending. This must be accompanied by concrete plans and designs to achieve a balanced budget (via a balanced budget amendment, spending cap, etc.). Many countries, including the United States, must identify governmental funding and spending structures that better balance current needs and obligations with those of future generations.[98]

Finally, a reemphasis of national unity over unquestioned allegiance to political party hierarchies and structures will be necessary. While party structures serve a purpose to align those with similar interests, in recent decades, they have become the equivalent of the tail that wags the dog. The win-at-all-costs, scorched-earth strategies employed by both parties have been on full display.

ECONOMIC

The solutions for the economy are large, global, and political. They may, therefore, seem outside our direct control and scope of influence. That being said, there are some philosophical frameworks that must be examined and hopefully considered.

While our capitalistic system is not designed or even desired to achieve income equality, it must be intended and perceived to afford equality of opportunity. The concepts of the American Dream and American exceptionalism were built around a constitutional (and capitalistic) structure that provided equality of opportunity to all who were citizens of this country. Most understand and acknowledge that such goals are aspirational, but recent events and social realities have demonstrated that we are many times perceived to fall short. While acknowledging our shortcomings, it is crucial that most participants in our democracy and economy understand the

[98] James Chen, "The Golden Rule of Government Spending," Investopedia.com, August 2020, https://www.investopedia.com/terms/g/golden-rule.asp.

structural opportunities and constraints of our capitalist and economic systems.[99]

A further improvement would focus on personal responsibility and education, particularly personal financial education. There are still vast swaths of our population who emerge from high schools, diplomas in hand, without ever having taken a class or been trained in fundamental personal and household financial management.[100] This lack of education and sophistication can lead people down unsustainable pathways from an early age, particularly from college to early adulthood.

Finally, consideration of moving our overall economy away from a dependence bordering on addiction to low interest rates, which benefit borrowers, and toward a more balanced and somewhat higher interest rate structure, which would begin to benefit savers and retirees. The current cheap-money economic system has forced too many savers, particularly retirees, to throw their hard-earned savings into riskier investments to earn realistic rates of return. This necessity of increasing risk can put savings, even retirement nest eggs, in increasing jeopardy.

SOCIETAL AND CULTURAL

Again, the issues faced in this dimension are far-reaching and will require long-range solutions as well as patience and

---

[99] "Is The American Dream Alive or Dead? It Depends on Where You Look," Economic Innovation Group, https://eig.org/dcieop.

[100] Liz Frazier, "5 Reasons Personal Finance Should Be Taught in School," Forbes.com, August 2019, https://www.forbes.com/sites/lizfrazierpeck/2019/08/29/5-reasons-personal-finance-should-be-taught-in-school/?sh=17ff23465178.

tolerance, all of which seem in short supply. There will need to be a bridging of gaps between political parties, media, and business interests so that all can work for the greater good. This will ultimately come down to leadership as coalitions of political, cultural, and business leaders emerge and work together to forge bonds across the divisions that currently exist.

It is increasingly apparent that addressing equality of opportunity via race, gender, and sexual identity, for example, will need to be central to these discussions. It seems that identifying and structuring long-term sustainable solutions in regard to immigration will be necessary as well. Ultimately, leaders will need to get people increasingly focused on what binds us versus those issues that continue to separate us.

It will be increasingly important to look to the past, and at previous decades and generations when we faced seemingly insurmountable challenges but were able to persevere and prosper. This American will and spirit continues to serve as the beacon that draws people to this country from all regions of the world.

GLOBAL

These largest and most complicated issues obviously will take a much more comprehensive and coordinated response. Additionally, many are not confined to one country. They are global in scope and will require wide-ranging solutions. Unfortunately, many of our global institutions (such as the UN and WHO) that have the capacity and scale are stressed, under assault, and in a state of transition. Increasingly, some regions and political associations now look at global structures and alliances with suspicion. The very institutions that will be central to identifying and managing such complexity find themselves weakened and somewhat destabilized.[101]

Some fear we are destined to go through a period of transition, possibly a global realignment, without the United States as leader and ultimate enforcement instrument. We will likely hit the wall in the coming decades before successfully identifying new global and national alliances that can help lay the needed foundations of trust and cooperation.

AN INDIVIDUAL ROAD MAP TO SUCCESS: 6E THINKING

While many of the macro issues identified are large and unwieldy, what we can do as individuals is more attainable. It is within our scope and control to move in positive directions, positioning our lives and careers for sustainability and success. Will this success resemble that of our parents and grandparents? Possibly not, but we can emerge with a life and career that is impactful, engaging, and worthwhile.

The framework of 6e Thinking can serve as a platform allowing for renewed focus and energy on key areas of importance. Concentrating on those issues and practices can help us sustainably navigate both our lives and careers through the perilous landscapes that lie ahead. I will now highlight and expand upon what such a framework will look like.

Resulting from our Promethean Life and Career Practices Model, the 6e Thinking framework encompasses an

[101] Rosemary DiCarlo, "Distrust of Public Institutions, Health Inequities Could Push More Countries into Conflict, UN Political Affairs Chief Warns," *UN News* (September 2020), https://news.un.org/en/story/2020/09/1072022.

understanding and acknowledgment that exponential change and convulsive environments will likely be the new normal. In that light, the following mental frameworks and practices will be crucial to surviving and thriving both personally and professionally in such challenging environments.

11
6E THINKING AND THE FIVE ANCHORS

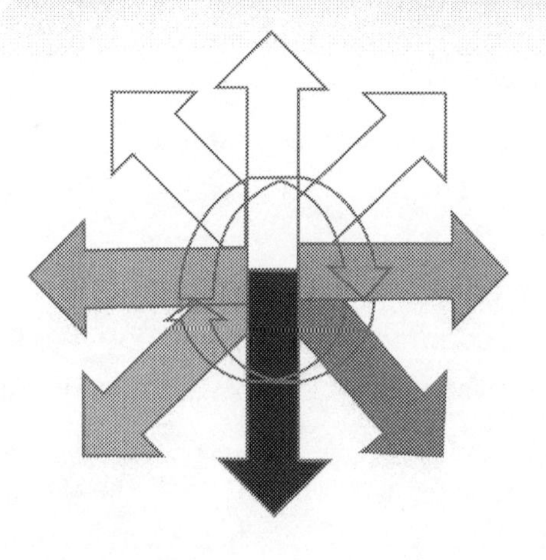

Straub/Researcher: Losing a job after fifteen years obviously left a lasting impression. What were your ultimate takeaways?

Research Participant: You know, I have thought about this a lot over the past six months, applying for jobs, hearing crickets … getting no action … eventually getting an interview now and then. It can be dehumanizing, depressing, and brutal … It kind of pissed me off at times …

Straub/Researcher: Why is that?

Research Participant: I have adult children and a grandchild on the way … and they are just lying to kids these days.

Straub/Researcher: How do you mean?"

Research Participant: There not preparing kids for what's coming, what they will have to deal with. They are pampered by their parents, by the schools, the media and advertisers pander to them … we tell them how great they are and how we are going to turn the world upside down to accommodate them.

I know this because that is what they told us as well. And then it seems to work that way for a while … and then life happens … reality hits.

I'm telling you … younger people … what they are coming into? They are going to have to position themselves better … they are going to have to learn how to take a punch.

I lost a job after fifteen years, lost my life … and it came out of nowhere! I felt like I got sucker-punched in the gut … it really set me back and made me question a lot of things about my life and career. Still not sure what to think at times.

Researcher Note: *This individual contacted me nine months after the initial interview. This is a partial record of that call and conversation.*

Straub/Researcher: Thank you for calling back with an update … I am so glad you were successful finding new employment. How are you feeling about your life and career currently?

Research Participant: Better ... no doubt about that. It is a very strong and stable company, I didn't have to relocate, and the pay and benefits are decent ... so it's all good ...

Straub/Researcher: I sense a *but* ...?

Research Participant: You know, it's funny. Everyone is really happy (almost euphoric) for me. And don't get me wrong ... I am very happy too.

But in many ways, I still feel traumatized by the experience. I've lost a sense of security, even innocence ... I don't know when (or if) I will ever get that back.

People think you are OK now ... but I'm not OK. I lost almost two years of income ... that is not OK. I am in my early forties, and I already feel my future plans for retirement are shredded. I had to deplete my savings and even dip into my 401K to get through this. I am a very good saver and financial planner ... I thought I was ready for anything ...

People will look at me in the next six months to a year and think everything is back to normal ... but I may never recover from this financially. I will tell you, this woke me up ... I will have contingencies for everything moving forward ... every type of scenario I can plan for.

I don't know if I will ever have that feeling of security again ... feel I can take anything for granted anymore. Who knows ... hopefully,

> this will be the one dramatic period in my life. I am cautiously hopeful and optimistic.

The five anchors of our 6e model should be visualized as those tools and practices that you can construct and develop in the external environment to help keep you (your boat) upright in tumultuous conditions. These are the five crucial practices that allow you to manage your career, risk profile, relational network, financial practices, and persistence/consistency of effort.

STRONG AND STABLE RELATIONSHIPS

This framework acknowledges and recognizes the importance of development, maintenance, and growth of relationships, understanding that connections and professional networks are necessary as well as a lifelong effort. This aspect of 6e Thinking highlights the importance of both weak-tie and strong-tie relationships. Further recognizing that family and community take many forms in current environments, the building of such support networks (in whatever form) is key to building and maintaining sustainable lives and careers.

One of the most striking differences we identified throughout our research studies was the positive impact of relational networks; the difference in outcomes between those who succeeded and those who failed was striking. This includes all forms of networks, although none is more important than family and community. There were numerous stories in our qualitative interviews where the very survival and recovery of individuals came down to strong family and relational connections. Communities were extremely important as well, whether actual towns and cities, churches, professional, virtual, or any number of other social groups. All proved important, in some cases critical, to success.

The size of the network proved important as well. An important fact that presented itself via our qualitative study was that in many cases, even weak-tie relationships were significant. In several cases, the individual who made the most difference (in attainment of another job or career) was someone totally unanticipated—a person many participants never would have suspected or predicted before their job loss.

6 KEYS FOR GROWTH AND DEVELOPMENT: RELATIONSHIPS

1. Personal and professional network-building
2. Generosity rather than keeping score in relationships
3. Good family relationships (in whatever form they take)
4. Prioritizing and investing in the relationships that matter
5. Maintaining and understanding the importance of weak-tie relationships
6. Investing in relationships for the long haul

ADAPTABILITY AND TOUGHNESS

Adaptability is defined as flexibility or the ability to adjust to different conditions. Internal locus of control is defined as the individual feeling that outcomes are controlled by your own personal decisions and efforts. In both our studies, those who enjoyed the greatest stability and success exhibited these two qualities. They could stick and move quickly and largely saw themselves as being in control of their own destiny. They were more pragmatic and tended to recover more quickly after a setback. They treated their life or career challenge as a temporary obstruction—and their recovery from it as their new full-time job.

Adaptability and internalization are crucial and can be learned, practiced, and employed in both your lives and careers. Both are mental frameworks involving being practical about potential realities and then positioning accordingly. While these skills for some seem rather natural, too often it is fantasy, denial, and avoidance that get in the way of moving in constructive and optimal directions.

With the convulsive and unpredictable conditions highlighted in this book, it will be necessary to be mentally tough and able to exhibit fortitude in the face of challenges. To succeed, survive, and even thrive in such environments, it will be necessary for each of us to toughen up and, figuratively speaking, be able to take a punch.

Recognizing the distinct possibility that those entering the workforce and even midcareer participants may have to reinvent themselves several times over the span of a normal life and career, finding support structures that enforce such new and desired mental frameworks is all-important. Equally significant can be suspending (at least temporarily) those associations that slow down or stall growth in these preferred directions. Commitment to adaptability and toughness is essential. Even though your external (displayed) confidence levels may not quite match up with actual realities, it is still crucial to push ahead projecting the confidence and toughness needed to persevere.

6 KEYS FOR GROWTH AND DEVELOPMENT: ADAPTABILITY AND TOUGHNESS

1. Understanding that change and adaptation will be crucial for sustainability and long-term success
2. Learning to (figuratively) take a punch
3. Learning to identify which issues and circumstances are within and outside of your direct control
4. Understanding that both adaptability and toughness are skills and competencies that can be learned and mastered
5. Learning to proactively research and identify issues and problems that might come your way
6. Understanding that convulsiveness and exponential change will likely be the new normal

FINANCIAL STEWARDSHIP

People with better outcomes in our study had the financial resources and savings to allow time to explore varied opportunities; additionally, it took pressure off their real-life circumstances, allowing them to focus on needed job-seeking tasks. This lack of immediate pressure allowed them to relax and display confidence during the job-search process as well as subsequent interview sessions. In our qualitative interviews, we noticed a distinct difference. Those not having such resources many times ended up taking jobs that were less than ideal, filling the desperate need to get a renewed income stream.

Some individuals who were especially successful engaged in lifetime earnings maximization; these people seemed less likely to lose jobs in the first place and were more adept at finding renewed career pathways in the event of a disruption in employment. They were quicker to identify when adjustments were needed (hours, income levels, and type of work) to keep existing jobs, as well as how best to position themselves to get back into the employment market before too much damage took place to future prospects and their financial future.

6 KEYS FOR GROWTH AND DEVELOPMENT: FINANCES

1. Employing the concepts of lifetime earnings maximization
2. Utilizing the tools of financial management (such as budgets)
3. Consistently utilizing professionals in the management of finances
4. Beginning the process of managing and planning finances early in your life and career
5. If possible, developing multiple income sources and streams
6. Utilizing a balanced, sustainable approach that prioritizes savings as well as personal and family enjoyment

PHYSICAL AND MENTAL VITALITY

Understanding that traditional life and career timelines are possibly forever changed, particularly retirement, we will have to be active and engaged careerists for longer periods of time. Physical and mental vibrancy will be necessary to allow us to remain engaged and meet family, career, and financial obligations.

There were noticeable career and life-outcome differences for those individuals who had taken their physical health and well-being seriously prior to (and after) the 2008 collapse. Those who had failed to do so were not as well positioned in relation to keeping or attaining jobs and careers in such a convulsive and competitive environment.

"There are fifty-year-olds … and there are fifty-year-olds." This quote from a study participant and employment placement professional sums up the subject at hand. She was making the point that physical vibrancy matters—for all ages. She further highlighted that those who failed to take their health, physical fitness, and overall well-being seriously could be at a stark disadvantage, particularly older workers in a more competitive and unstable job market. This sentiment was echoed throughout our qualitative interviews and was backed up by our quantitative study as well—all levels, from placement professionals to employers to those seeking jobs backed up this important finding.

6 KEYS FOR GROWTH AND DEVELOPMENT: VITALITY

1. Developing and employing physical fitness plans and regimens
2. Understanding the importance of mental acuity and what contributes to it
3. Understanding that physical and mental vitality contribute to attainment and sustainability of employment relationships
4. Maintaining top levels of mental engagement

5. Regular engagement with health regimens and professionals (such as yearly checkups and assessments)
6. Understanding that lifelong learning and skill attainment will be hallmarks of mental vitality and longevity

LIFELONG LEARNING

Learning can be defined as "acquiring new or modifying existing knowledge, behaviors, skills, preferences or values." However you define it, understanding its importance is significant. Thinking of the brain as like any other muscle in your body can be a helpful comparative. It must be stretched and worked to strengthen it, and neglect of this process will lead to weakening, even atrophy. While seemingly self-evident, the value of learning and skills development cannot be overestimated when it comes to the difference of outcomes of those who took part in my study.

There are several types of educational attainment available to most individuals; I will highlight three types of learning that I feel are of particular importance. First is *skills maintenance and development*. This can take several forms, from general personal enrichment to company- or industry-specific skills to more explicit professional development (such as for a CPA, law, or medicine) that involves licensing and technical skills updates. Second is *traditional formalized education attainment*. This could come in the form of technical/trade schools to community colleges and finally university educational settings. Third is the training needed for individuals who are *building or adding skills in a different field or industry*, possibly due to a job dislocation or even a post-retirement career evolution.

Those in my study who continued their learning had much-improved transitions and outcomes. The process of reengaging and reintegrating via different circumstances seemed in some ways an ordinary offshoot of their ongoing educational and growth processes.

6 KEYS FOR GROWTH AND DEVELOPMENT: LEARNING

1. Understanding the relationship between continued learning and skill development as it relates to career success and sustainability
2. Understanding the different forms of learning and skill development as well as their value to life and professional development
3. Understanding the importance of mental vitality
4. Understanding the different types of learning models and access (such as traditional education, online or in person)
5. Understanding the linkage of lifelong learning with social relationships and general well-being
6. Understanding the multigenerational influence your educational patterns set for children, grandchildren and others that look to you for guidance

6 KEY TAKEAWAYS: THE FIVE ANCHORS

1. It is crucial to understand the importance of strong and stable relationships.
2. The importance of adaptability and toughness will be key in more convulsive environments.
3. The importance of financial stewardship can be illustrated by skill attainment in such topics.
4. The importance of physical and mental vitality will be key to career longevity.
5. The importance of lifelong learning will be key to career sustainability.
6. Paying attention to the six key areas of growth and development for each of the above is important.

12
6E THINKING AND THE THREE PRACTICES

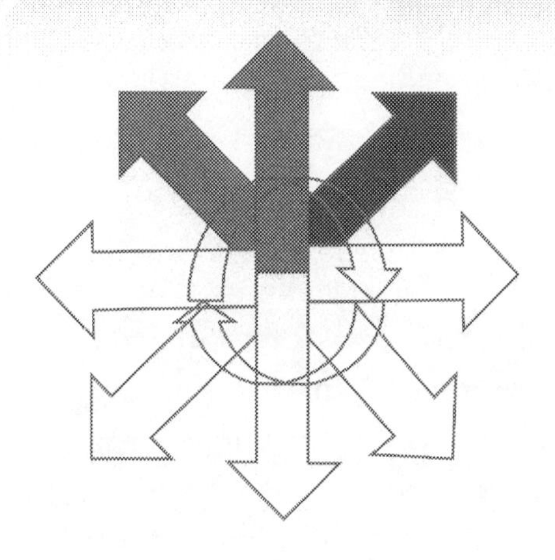

Research Participant: I grew up watching *Star Trek* as a kid, and I was enthralled with the multilevel chess game that Spock would play. That is what life is like now; you have to plan for and position for multiple realities. Thank God we did that … it is what saved our bacon when I lost my job.

Straub/Researcher: Who is *we*?

> **Research Participant:** Sorry ... my wife and I. We are both planners, we think a lot about the what-ifs ...
>
> We are both obsessive about keeping our networks strong and vibrant, same with our skills ... continuing to get educated ...
>
> Also, every six months, we would do intellectual exercises ... almost like two-minute drills in football. My wife and I would imagine different scenarios—if I lost my job, if she lost hers, or if we both lost our jobs ...
>
> We would play out what we would do and how we would move toward recovery. What our budgets would look like ... those sorts of things. We have always positioned our life and expense structure on being able to live (for the most part) on either one of our salaries.
>
> One of the key things that came out of that role-playing was that speed and flexibility would be crucial. You have to move quickly, and you better have a plan. You better not dwell on what used to be ... better figure out your new reality and build your different future based on your current circumstances, budgets, networks, support systems, etc. Then work the plan ...
>
> The pre-planning and positioning we did really paid off with this recent (extended) layoff ... We were ready.

We will highlight the three key practices in regards to 6 e Thinking, they are scenario planning, positivity and practicality.

SCENARIO PLANNING

This aspect of the three practices can be viewed as playing on multiple chessboards at once—and not knowing which game is the one that actually counts. Those who were successful and rebounded more quickly were individuals who had acknowledged and planned for multiple possible realities, providing themselves with options based on different realities that might present themselves in the course of their lives and careers.

These individuals managed their lives and careers like a portfolio of possibilities. Their ultimate tools were those of risk assessment, analysis, and management. They further recognized that they could not and would not make correct decisions all the time. There would be mistakes; however, they were consistent in regard to getting as much quality information and data as possible, hopefully leading to a higher percentage of optimal decisions and outcomes.

Those who succeeded thought multi-dimensionally about their risk profile, looking at personal, family, career, societal, and macroeconomic factors. In their personal assessments, they did well at balancing their individual and family needs as well as the needs of their larger environments. When assessing societal and macroeconomic factors, they looked at the health of public and private institutions, pension systems, the type of asset categories they personally should invest in (housing, cash, equities, precious metals), prospective industry health, even location and regional strength.

6 KEYS FOR GROWTH AND DEVELOPMENT: SCENARIO PLANNING

1. Utilization of recognized risk-management tools
2. Conducting of scenario analysis and establishing risk-management profiles
3. Understanding that risk-management profiles need to be reviewed and updated periodically
4. Understanding that multiple realities may need to be considered when moving forward in lives and careers (multiple chessboards)
5. Trying to keep multiple pathways, even income streams, in play when possible
6. Acknowledging that if hyper convulsive environments and exponential change are indeed the new normal, this type of adaptability will be crucial to life and career sustainability

POSITIVITY

Positivity is defined as the practice and tendency of being positive or optimistic in one's approach. This framework was exhibited in many instances throughout our study. Many of our research participants understood the importance of having a positive framework and mental model. Furthermore, they utilized the tools of growth, including education, social engagement, mental discipline, and physical maintenance.

It is essentially important to understand and ensure that your mental health and positive framework are ultimately within your control and not dependent on other individuals. Finally, our participants understood that this was a long-term process, with wins and setbacks. Many employed resiliency and toughness to overcome short-term challenges while keeping a disciplined eye on their ultimate objectives.

6 KEYS FOR GROWTH AND DEVELOPMENT: POSITIVITY

1. Avoiding negative impacts and influences on one's life and career when possible, whether this be individuals, activities, or groups
2. Identifying and utilizing positive yet accurate information sources
3. Identifying and embracing mentors who serve as good role models for the desired framework, behaviors, and outcomes
4. Embracing mental and physical practices that lead to an improved sense of well-being
5. Taking concrete actions in your career to contribute to more fulfilling and enjoyable work environments
6. Finding opportunities to engage with the natural environment as well as the attainment of spiritual growth

PRACTICALITY

Practicality is defined quite simply as the "state of being practical."[102] This is the tool of employing realism in key aspects of lives and careers. Learn to utilize the tools of research and risk analysis to assess each personal and professional situation. Understand the importance of employing networks and mentors,

[102] Cambridge Dictionary, s.v. "practicality," accessed May 6, 2021, https://dictionary.cambridge.org/us/dictionary/english/practicality.

both personal and professional, to help with assessments and calculations of identified potential risks and rewards.

It can be helpful to associate with like-minded individuals who can serve as mentors and colleagues—this to help with assessing reality and determining optimal decisions and solutions. Inversely, it can also be beneficial to have those in your network who come at decisions and analysis from a contrarian, even pessimistic perspective, providing balance to analysis and decisions.

6 KEYS FOR GROWTH AND DEVELOPMENT: PRACTICALITY

1. Objectively assessing your abilities and limitations—physical, emotional, and career
2. Objectively assessing your ambitions in regard to your life and career
3. Establishing clear and rational goals for your life
4. Objectively assessing and evaluating your expectations of those around you, including family, friends, and professional associates
5. Constantly reassessing your abilities, goals, ambitions, and relationships
6. Seeking out mentors who can help you understand your attributes and weaknesses, and assist in evaluating life and career realities

6 KEY TAKEAWAYS: THE THREE PRACTICES

1. This chapter keys on the three practices of the 6e Thinking model. These elements highlight particular actions and frameworks that build on the solid foundations provided by the five anchors of the model.
2. Scenario planning involves mapping and planning different alternatives in lives and careers based on varied possibilities and outcomes.
3. Winning at the game of life many times takes playing more than one chess game at a time, needing to play them all to win.
4. Positivity involves utilizing positive forward-looking frameworks in managing lives and careers.
5. Practicality involves utilizing a realistic perspective and outlook in managing lives and career options, challenges, and opportunities.
6. Positivity and practicality are identifiable skills that can be learned, practiced, and applied to life and career practices and outcomes.

13

6E THINKING AND LIFE AND CAREER TRANSFORMATION

Research Participant: My wife and I talked after my layoff and decided it was time for me to make a definitive change … This was my third forced career change in the last fifteen years.

I was done with this … the corporate merry-go-round, the old version of myself … Goodbye, old Daniel … hello, new Daniel.

> We did not talk about what we lost; we looked at what we stood to gain. We had savings, good retirement portfolios. She still had a steady job and stable income stream. We were looking toward a new and reimagined version of our lives and careers.
>
> Even though we were both in our early fifties, we knew we wanted to work at least another twenty years plus. We were in good health … The kids were graduated from college.
>
> It was a rejuvenation of sorts. It was like we were young newlyweds again … ready to take on the world … us against them.

Those in my study (who succeeded) ultimately viewed their career as something in a state of perpetual evolution and even somewhat boundary less. They were realistic and understood that their career would possibly take them through different jobs, companies, and maybe even industries; but they maintained a sense of control while managing their career developments and direction. These individuals did not take their jobs for granted; rather, they valued and did their best to maintain their jobs (when considered mutually beneficial).

A longer-term focus and outlook emerged from those who achieved better outcomes, with many viewing their longer-term goals and objectives as being much more important than what happened in the recent past. One described viewing a career like a rock-climbing wall rather than a traditional ladder that always leads up; at times, lateral or even downward career moves might be required to take care of longer-term goals and professional objectives.

Those who were finding success were much more realistic

about their career temporal window. They understood that they might need to work longer (delaying retirement) to ensure ultimate and long-term success, even attaining residual secondary employment when needed. These individuals seemed pragmatic; some were even skeptical about the prospect of ultimately receiving all the retirement benefits promised by governments and institutions.

One study participant conveyed a personal story. This individual had recently had a medical stent put in for a partially blocked artery at the age of sixty, noting that his father had a very similar issue at his age thirty years earlier. He noted that at the time of his father's occurrence, there was little doctors could do but tell him to "Take it easy, eat right, and get your affairs in order." His father ultimately died at of a heart attack at age sixty-five. The research participant is now seventy-five and in great health, highlighting that he has made good on his extra time, continuing to work part-time, volunteer, and be a productive part of society.

Many in my study who survived and prospered were planning to work longer than the traditional retirement age. Some were positioned for and getting trained for their second (or even third) career. Another interesting finding was that many viewed their earning potential in the same light: what we refer to as *lifetime earnings maximization*. In some cases, they were open to stagnant or even reduced income levels in an effort to keep their long-term employment prospects healthy and intact.

People who exhibited this type of career flexibility and adaptability had much-improved outcomes over those who did not. In almost all cases, these were not reactionary moves but well-considered, disciplined, and designed to take care of the long-term interests of their family, finances, and career. Those who displayed this profile were also likely to be much more flexible with regard to retirement planning.

6 KEYS FOR GROWTH AND DEVELOPMENT: LIFE AND CAREER TRANSFORMATION

1. Developing and constantly renewing a personal and professional mission statement
2. Developing and constantly renewing personal and professional goals and ambitions
3. Developing and constantly reevaluating key and relevant timelines with regard to your life and career
4. Investing in what matters most—family, health, and overall well-being
5. Investing in the lives and careers of those in your circle of influence, understanding that this will serve as the ultimate foundation of your continued and ongoing sustainability
6. Consistently and regularly taking the time to unplug from technology as well as recharging and rejuvenating your mind, body and soul

While no model offers a guarantee for success, this framework could well provide the best odds for positive outcomes and stability throughout life and career horizons. Further, it can serve as a potential blueprint for future generations, as they search for more sustainable structures and patterns in personal, organizational and societal frameworks.

6 KEY TAKEAWAYS: LIFE AND CAREER TRANSFORMATION

1. Prioritize lifetime earnings maximization.
2. Prioritize lifelong learning and skill development.
3. Plan to work longer if necessary.
4. Value and invest in physical and mental pursuits.
5. Understand that crafting and maintaining a relevant, updated and utilized personal mission statement can be a key to sustainable growth and development.
6. Understand that career advancement and sustainability may involve career mapping, including upward, lateral, and even downward movements.

THE FIFTH CONVULSION:
THE SALE OF THE BUSINESS AND WHAT'S NEXT?

COMPONENTS OF 6E THINKING

- scenario planning
- adaptability and toughness
- practicality
- positivity
- financial management

In the previous segment of our story, I highlighted the phase of our company history that I termed *riding the dragon*—the period that encompassed the rise of sales levels to potentially unsustainable heights. While there were concerns about this fast growth, there was also significant pressure on dealers to make sure representative market shares were attained during this unlikely bull-market run in the industry. Had we not attained a representative share of this abundance, our manufacturers would have been very unforgiving, and understandably so.

In respect to such realities and forces, the decision was made to stretch out our organizational structures and increase our sales and corresponding debt levels—taking the harrowing ride up the industry roller-coaster. As is many times the case, next came the corresponding drop as the market softened and conditions became less favorable to the industry. This was no surprise, as our dealership group and most others had planned for this downturn; even the timing of it was somewhat expected. What was unexpected was the intensity, both in scale and quickness. Over the span of three years, sales dropped to half of their peak levels.

Most in the industry, including manufacturers and economists, had expected a more gradual and sustained decline over about a five-to seven-year period. The downturn we experienced was breathtaking in its scope and increasingly difficult to weather. It became evident early on that many dealers, including us, would struggle greatly in the face of these new and dramatic conditions. Over the course of the following five-year period, we would fight to restructure our business for the new conditions and realities we faced—to position our company for an increasingly volatile industry landscape.

During this period, and with our manufacturer's guidance and support, we made the difficult decision to close two of our seven stores, consolidating market coverage within the remaining five. These moves were received well in the market, and we were able to retain the majority of the business in those market areas, utilizing delivery enticements and flexible field-service options.

However, over the course of this same period, it became increasingly evident to both our company and our primary manufacturer that our organizational and capitalization structure would likely not be able to keep pace with the industry changes and requirements. It was at this point that we began the process of working with our key stakeholders to explore exit strategies involving the sale of the business.

During this re-evaluation process, a primary goal was to protect the structure and ongoing market presence of the business. This we were able to do successfully. A particular challenge with the sale of the business was that early on, it became evident that we would not be able to keep the impending sale of our company a secret, to either employees or customers. In an age of technology and social media, it was just not realistic. The sale would take close to a year to transact and require access by the purchasing company to our assets, market data, select customers, and employees.

With that realization, nine months before the actual sale would finalize, we had to do the unthinkable: pull back the curtain and tell all of our employees and customers what we expected to transpire—the potential sale of the company. We gave them all the facts while making them aware there was still a significant chance the sale might not finalize. While this provided much uncertainty for our organization and its stakeholders, the relationships we had built through the previous decades with our employees, customers, and suppliers paid off incredibly well. During this period, we did not have one significant defection of either employees or customers. Both stakeholder groups felt confident that we would do our best to safeguard their interests in the process of selling the business.

While we went through the process of selling the company, we had to work at balancing the needs of all of our stakeholder groups. In addition to employees and customers, there were minority stockholders, suppliers, and entire communities that needed these dealerships to be in operation and sustainable. Additionally, there were the next-generation family members who had invested the last decade-plus of their careers in the company. Finally, there were the principle stockholders: my brother, my sister-in-law, and myself.

We felt positive that if we could sell the company successfully, most employees would have the opportunity to move forward and be employed with the successor company. Additionally, our next-generation family members were very talented and well positioned via the professional experiences, training, and contacts they had gained during their tenure with the organization. My brother and his wife were well positioned for retirement. My wife's and my situation was a bit more tenuous; in our mid- to late fifties, it would be more interesting for us to get situated appropriately and position our careers moving forward. It was during this period that all of the preplanning and positioning would pay off, allowing us all to move forward with attractive and engaging career possibilities.

In the final analysis, the process of the transaction could not have gone much better. Yes, it was intense, and at times there were hurt feelings and even disagreements. But through it all, we worked together, finding the optimal and most equitable ways through these challenges while keeping our eye on the ultimate desired and needed conclusion: the sale of the company.

14

6E THINKING AND BRINGING IT ALL TOGETHER

Researcher Note: *As a student of how people manage lives and careers in convulsive environments, I talk about my research regularly. While discussing my study casually at the Glidden House Hotel (Cleveland, Ohio) with fellow doctoral students, a patron sitting close by overheard parts of our conversation. He came up to me shortly after my fellow students left for a dinner engagement and asked if he could learn more about my doctoral investigation.*

After we had talked for about half an hour, he said he had a story that might be of interest. This individual had lost employment a few years earlier at approximately forty-three years of age. While he eventually succeeded in replacing the lost job with a very good position and opportunity, he was out of work for almost a year. This interchange highlights the last part of that very impactful conversation.

Straub/Researcher: Tell me with as much detail as you care to provide … what you experienced and felt throughout this interesting and very intense period of your life.

Research Participant: You know … I guess at the end of the day, I'm pretty proud of myself and my family.

Straub/Researcher: Can you elaborate?

Research Participant: Sure … Well, I feel like we took about everything this f**king world … you said I could say what I want … this f**king world could throw at us. Not only are we still standing … I think we are all much stronger because of it.

Straub/Researcher: How so?

Research Participant: In about every way possible. Our kids are better people … they got a real dose of reality … had to grow up a little quicker … not so spoiled anymore.

We had to pull together as a family. My wife and I have a much better and more honest relationship.

We stayed home more, spent time together, home movie nights … not so many people around … not so many distractions.

Straub/Researcher: Can you give me five words that describe that period of your life?

Research Participant: Intense. Scary. Suicide. Reflection. Rejuvenation. Growth … Oops—I guess that is six? And pretty much in that order …

Straub/Researcher: Suicide?

Research Participant: To clarify … and not to be overly dramatic … it was not seriously considered …

My son is very good with technology. I was going through a particularly dark time about five months in (as we discussed, it took about eleven months for me to find my current job). My son—I think he was worried about me … well, he must have hacked my computer password and was looking at my Google searches. *Best ways to commit suicide* showed up as one of my queries.

Straub/Researcher: What did your son do with that information?

Research Participant: He was a freshman in high school and his brother was still in middle school … He shared it with his younger brother. They obviously did not know what to do …

They did the smart thing and showed it to their mother … Then there was a family intervention (my wife and two sons). My wife, my sons, and I spent a couple hours together …

talking. They just assured me we were in this together and we would get through all of this together.

It was so touching, impactful, and beautiful. And it worked ... I didn't feel judged ... feel like a failure ... I didn't feel alone anymore.

I did feel ashamed, though ... that I was even thinking about giving up ... I felt like a coward.

Straub/Researcher: Wow ... what a story ... what a family!

Research Participant: You have no idea! My wife got a better (full-time) job during this period to help out ... My sons got me involved in helping them start a lawn-care business ... We would mow lawns together on evenings and weekends. They still operate that little company to this day, and I still help them with it when I can.

You want to know the ultimate irony ... I struck up a friendship with one of the people we were mowing for regularly. He worked for and ended up having quite a bit to do with me getting the job at the company I am working for now.

This research interview highlights a very significant reality: times of transition bring great opportunity and great risk, times of hopefulness and times of fear, times of jubilation and even times of desperation. This is the reality that we all potentially face. There is no getting around it.

Our lives are not movies or novels that we get to experience and enjoy with detached amusement. Such challenges put a family's security and livelihood at stake, and unlike with a good book or movie, we can't assume or necessarily anticipate a happy ending. My family and I went through the same challenges, the same uncertainty—the not knowing. Not knowing how the reality of our business and eventual sale of our company would turn out was excruciating, even terrifying at times.

Throughout these dynamic periods, we employed key models and frameworks that guided our actions and led to more positive outcomes. I will examine a few of these strategies and also highlight briefly how they tie in with the 6e Thinking framework that I have proposed.

THE IMPORTANCE OF WEAK-TIE RELATIONSHIPS

Our model notes the importance of networks. Both my family members and I had strong personal and professional networks, and we utilized them to the fullest. Interestingly, many of us were greatly aided by people who would be characterized as weak-tie relationships. In my research, I heard the same theme repeatedly: *the person who ended up making the most difference in my reemployment was the person I would have least expected.* Many of us had similar circumstances. It wasn't the people you would have necessarily predicted who had the most impact on your outcomes.

This reemphasizes the importance of strong, sizeable, and flourishing networks. There is much negative publicity surrounding social networks, but they are key to laying a good personal and career foundation that can be utilized during times of opportunity as well as professional difficulty.

TIME TO EXECUTE STRATEGIES AND TIME TO HEAL

Time can be an important ally or a cruel taskmaster. After a job separation, there are many needs for time: time to heal, time to analyze and accept the new reality, time to learn, time to plan, and finally time to execute a strategy for moving forward.

One of my family members had not been successful at the six-month mark in attaining another job, despite working hard and interviewing regularly. The right job had been elusive to that point. I discussed the importance of the next six months (in the statistics of job attainment for those over fifty, the prospects after being out of a job for more than a year are bleak).[103] He stumbled upon something that was quite intriguing: an opportunity to work in Louisiana at the site of the Exon Valdez oil spill over monthly (intermittent) cycles and then be back home for alternating months. The earnings would give him additional time to search, but more importantly, this job would hit the pause button on the out-of-work time clock. It worked amazingly well. Potential employers seemed impressed at the lengths he would go to take care of his family and other personal obligations.

Healing many times happens in two forms. Initially, many of those suddenly separated from jobs feel a sense of loss, failure, and even betrayal. I will never forget talking to a participant in my research study who had been terminated via a mass layoff event of over two hundred employees due to a significant slowdown in the economy. Despite being one of hundreds

[103] Peter Gosselin, "If You're Over 50, Chances Are the Decision to Leave a Job Won't Be Yours," ProPublica.org, December 2018, https://www.propublica.org/article/older-workers-united-states-pushed-out-of-work-forced-retirement.

forcibly separated from a job that week, this individual still felt bitter, personally targeted, and betrayed by the company. Next, she was additionally devastated at being separated from her work family of over ten years without any sense of closure or opportunity of continued relational structures. No goodbyes, no going-away parties, just a long painful walk out of the building—accompanied by company security.

THE IMPORTANCE OF KEEPING SKILLS AND KNOWLEDGE CURRENT

In my particular instance, the importance of keeping skills and knowledge current proved critical, much as our model would have predicted. I was fortunate to be able to update and attain several higher-education degrees and designations, culminating in the earning of my doctoral degree. Additionally, I had taught for several universities, teaching many different classes and most importantly embracing online learning platforms. These skills kept my instructional and technology skills relevant, up-to-date, and at optimal proficiencies.

THE CONCEPT AND IMPORTANCE OF INTELLECTUAL ACCOUNTABILITY

Much research has shown the connection between being intellectually active and the continued vitality of the brain.[104] In highlighting what I refer to as *intellectual accountability*, I take this a step further. It is my suspicion that traditional retirement is not always the best alternative, and that decreased

---

[104] Dr. Sanjay Gupta, "Tips to Keep Your Brain Healthy from Dr. Sanjay Gupta," CNN.com, January 2021, https://www.youtube.com/watch?v=i3O5zFm1yck.

activity and stimulation of our brain and neuro pathways is not necessarily a sustainable or desired state. Studies show that doing puzzles, volunteering, and remaining socially active can be good tools for intellectual maintenance. However, being intellectually (even physically) accountable for results might prove an even better mechanism.

Being accountable for deadline-driven and definable results encourages the brain to maintain workable neuro pathways. It has been shown that during the course of our lives, most of us suffer numerous mini strokes (TIA), many of which we are not acutely aware of. These events shows up regularly in autopsies and the inspection of brains post mortem.[105] Being intellectually accountable, I hypothesize, forces our brains to reroute our neuro pathways out of necessity, constantly building reworked and rerouted transmission and networked corridors.

This intellectual accountability could take many forms: working longer, a dissimilar post-retirement career (with possibly less stress and strain), or vigorous volunteering opportunities with defined responsibilities and opportunities for intellectual stimulation and social engagement. According to the recent book *Keep Sharp: Build a Better Brain at Any Age* by Sanjay Gupta, physical exercise, intellectual stimulation, and engagement is the same as signaling to the brain "Hey, I am still here and in the game." This is very important and foundational to long, quality, and rewarding lives.[106]

---

[105] "Transient Ischemic Attack (TIA)," Mayoclinic.org, https://www.mayoclinic.org/diseases-conditions/transient-ischemic-attack/symptoms-causes/syc-20355679.

[106] Sanjay Gupta, *Keep Sharp, Build a Better Brain at Any Age* (New York: Simon and Schuster, 2021).

LIFETIME EARNINGS MAXIMIZATION

Finally, with all of this as our foundation, comes the concept of *lifetime earnings maximization*, or taking care of long-term prospects and sustainability of careers, possibly at the expense of our short-term interests. Delaying retirement, taking new positions to spur growth and expertise, and taking care of ourselves physically are all crucial in regard to this important strategy. We have to play the long game to be successful in both our lives and our careers.

Sadly, some participants in my research studies did not have successful conclusions. There were many challenging situations and stories. However, there were others who had done many things correctly to prepare for potential career disruptions. Their stories were no doubt much more encouraging. What made the most significant impression throughout was that there were no out-of-the-park home runs. It was simply a matter of doing the little things right throughout their lives, consistently and with planned intent.

This final observation particularly aligns with our model and the direction it gives to career professionals. Doing all of the unglamorous but important things and having the right mindset will put you in the best position for success and allow you the best chance to maximize your career prospects as well as lifetime earnings capabilities.

6 KEY TAKEAWAYS: BRINGING IT ALL TOGETHER

1. Family communication and support is critical in times of career disruption.
2. Weak tie relationships can be vitally important in securing new career opportunities.
3. After job separation it is important to take time to heal before seeking re- employment.
4. Work to keep skills and knowledge current while looking for replacement employment.
5. Understand that lifetime learning as well as intellectual growth and engagement are key.
6. Understand that lifetime earnings maximization must be balanced with short term needs.

THE SIXTH CONVULSION: REINVENTION—NEW PATHWAYS AND NEW BEGINNINGS

COMPONENTS OF 6E THINKING

- physical and mental vitality
- adaptability and toughness
- practicality
- lifelong learning
- strong and stable relationships
- life and career management
- financial management

It is interesting, and a bit ironic, that in most instances when a business is sold, those selling the company tend to be congratulated for their success; it's viewed as the ultimate capstone to their entrepreneurial endeavor. While it is easiest and most tempting to feed into this very accommodating narrative, in most cases, it is much more complicated than what is conveniently portrayed. I have found myself very quick to accept laudatory statements from friends, family, and colleagues—but in our case, as with many others, the truth is more nuanced.

While we knew and acknowledged that what eventually happened was a distinct possibility, we still had hoped and intended for this business to go on well into the future. This is the reason we had brought next-generation family members into the organization and had invested millions of dollars building the business, the facilities, and the markets that they served. This also was the reason we ultimately entered seven markets throughout the Midwest.

Make no mistake—we had hoped to continue on with the business. Even five years earlier, it had appeared that we were well positioned not only to accomplish this objective but also to grow the business and company into a twenty-plus-store multistate dealership-management company. Then life happened: a rapidly shifting agricultural economy changed plans and moved us to the sidelines as the overall industry convulsed, consolidated, and repositioned. Suddenly, and in the span of less than five years, we went from having an inside-track seat at the table to finding ourselves on the outside looking in.

That being acknowledged, we had in many other ways been planning for this alternate reality, just as surely as we had planned for the other (growth, survival, even ascendancy). One of the driving reasons we moved into the multistore-ownership realm initially was because we knew it would make our business more attractive and saleable if the need were to arise. We identified potential markets and made real estate and asset investments based on this very real possibility and alternative possible outcome.

So when this reality presented itself, we were ready. We had been planning for this less-desirable eventuality our entire careers. As referenced earlier, we viewed our business and careers as having multiple chess games going at once, without us knowing which game counted; in this respect, it was crucial that we play them all to win. This is how we strategically positioned, planned, and managed our operations. This is why we were ready for what came next, no matter what the eventual outcome.

This period and the sale of the business was no doubt one of the most challenging times in our family's history and professional experience. There were multiple levels to work on simultaneously. At times, it seemed the options were chosen from a drop-down menu of least-worst choices.

There were also the emotions within the family as well as those of long-term employees of the company. Gloss it over as you will, there were hurt feelings, even at times bordering on feelings of betrayal within the family and from some stakeholders. We communicated and then communicated some more, trying to bring everyone along to a point of understanding—an acceptance of why and how we were doing what we were doing.

Overall, it was felt that the process went well, or as well as could be expected. As noted, we did not lose one key employee and we lost very few business or individual customer or supplier relationships. Had both (or either) happened, it could have derailed the sale of the company and threatened the survival of the organization.

So yes, the sale of our business by most measures should be deemed a success: we got an acceptable price, and most employees (who wished to) remained employed with the purchasing company and are doing very well. Those who did not move on with the purchasing company did so at their own choosing and in almost all cases found solid and comparable employment to move their careers forward.

My brother and sister-and-law were both able to successfully retire, separately helping their daughter Kristy transition into a successful residual business. I was able to find engaging and very solid employment as a professor at a university. My wife is still employed with the organization that purchased our business.

In some ways, as I look back on this experience, I cannot help but view it somewhat comparatively with the "Miracle on the Hudson." We took a very challenging, even potentially catastrophic situation and were able to make the best of a violent reality, successfully landing our "plane" in treacherous conditions, with no loss of life (careers and livelihoods) and very little collateral damage. In the end, all bills were paid, and we extracted as much value as possible for the stockholders of the company.

When I teach entrepreneurial management courses, one thing University and midcareer students ask me is: "Is it worth it? Owning a business? Taking the risks and everything else that goes with it?"

The answer I give them is this: "It is … but be very aware of the risks as well as your tolerance of risk, uncertainty, and stress."

Despite everything we went through and experienced, I wouldn't change any of it—the opportunity to experience everything we did while working with family and the wonderful people who made up the core of our organization, industry, and customer segment. Absolutely, I think most of us would take that ride, take that chance again. It is in many ways the American dream as well as the American experience.

CALL TO ACTION

The big lie in this whole thing … is that we've got this sensible country with a dysfunctional Washington … The reality is we have a country of people who want to bankrupt their children (and grandchildren) to spend money on themselves—and they will punish any politician who prevents them from doing that.—***David Brooks, NY Times columnist, Meet the Press, December 30, 2012***

This quote seems a good place to end our dialog. It's the closest this author has seen to a top-level official or pundit in Washington, DC, actually telling the truth about our current state of affairs. This kind of brutal honesty is needed now more than ever to survive times such as I have highlighted within the course of our journey.

As evidenced by exponential technological innovation, globalization, and speed-of-light economic and societal transformations, we are moving into a realm and landscape that will be very different from that faced by our parents and grandparents. A new model will be needed to guide us through this exciting and potentially perilous terrain. This research and the resultant 6e Thinking framework has been my attempt to help imagine and define what that new paradigm and pathway might resemble.

Truth and accountability will be crucial, and ultimately an understanding that we have all been part of bringing our economic and societal structures to this point and we will all need to do our part to help resolve these historic and unprecedented challenges. This can only be accomplished by building personal, family, business, and community configurations in a new way that will allow us to join forces while we collectively conquer and weather the storms that come our way.

I hope this book has provided insights and encouragement to help move you forward on your personal and professional journey. I wish you the best of luck and good fortune as you proceed through the interesting times that will surely present themselves in the coming decades.

6 KEY TAKEAWAYS: CALL TO ACTION

1. We have to look within as well as without for answers, dealing with and positioning for increasingly convulsive environments.
2. Positioning oneself high on the proverbial watchtower and constantly scanning for and understanding emerging environments will be crucial. What worked before may not work in the future.
3. It will be necessary to constantly develop and evolve skills and abilities.
4. We must think multi-dimensionally, valuing the interests of both current and future generations.
5. We must constantly assess and develop our personal and professional support networks.
6. We must assess and reassess our career timelines and landscapes, taking care of ourselves physically and mentally so that we can work as long as necessary.

APPENDIX A
THE PROMETHEAN MEASUREMENT TOOL

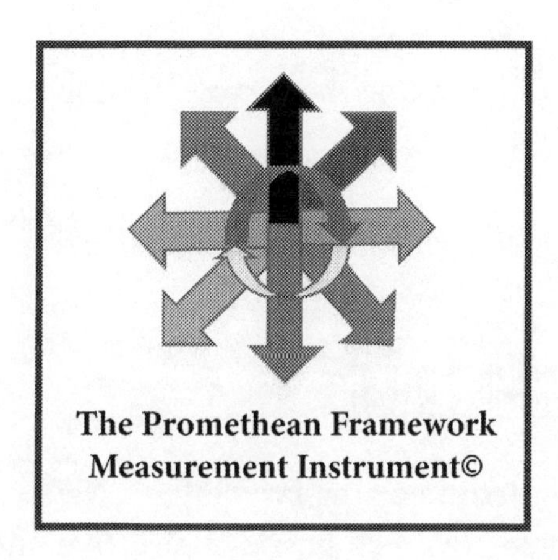

INTRODUCTION

We live in increasingly dynamic and polarized times, as witnessed by world events like the increasing rise of terrorism, the meltdown of many significant economic institutions, political polarization and populism, and major environmental concerns relating to climate change. As economies and societies exhibit distress from fractured political, academic, health, and economic systems, we feel we will witness increasing levels of convulsiveness in our institutions, markets, and public foundations. How prepared are you to weather such times in relation to your life and career?

THE PROMETHEAN MEASUREMENT TOOL

This measurement tool is designed to help individuals measure their ability to sustain and even thrive in convulsive economies and societies. The seventy-three-question survey is intended to be taken in a single sitting and should take approximately twenty minutes to complete

Please consider taking the survey, the link can be accessed at the author's website:

http://larrystraub.com/

CONVULSIVE ECONOMIC QUOTIENT

This quotient, derived by the Promethean Measurement Tool, produces a predictive composite figure that measures your unique ability to survive and prosper in pronounced convulsive economic cycles. Each of the nine components in the model (Appendix B) produces an individual component score along with the combined CEQ score for the entire tool / survey.

The table provided for analysis will show where an individual exhibits gaps or deficiencies, and this should serve as a road map for future directions for growth. A score of 80 percent or greater is very good; a score between 60 to 80 percent is good;

and a score of 60 percent and under indicates a deficiency that needs attention.

We hope this measurement tool will provide insights and understanding in regard to your abilities and prospects to withstand the increasingly convulsive environments that might present themselves in the coming decades.

APPENDIX B
PROMETHEAN FRAMEWORK AND MEASUREMENT INSTRUMENT - GROUPS AND COMPONENTS

GROUP: CONCEPTUAL FRAMEWORK

A. ***Ability to Adapt (and Locus of Control)***: Identifies an individual's perception of control in relation to life and career, and additionally, the fortitude the individual has in terms of altering/impacting negative directions in life and career.

B. ***Persistence and Consistency of Effort***: Demonstrates an individual's consistency of effort and fortitude in the face of both opportunities and challenges. This innate ability will impact the individual's capacity to both retain current employment and attract or attain new employment in the case of job loss or career disruption.

C. ***Career Timeline***: This measurement speaks to an individual's flexibility in relation to the career/ retirement timeline. A more elastic timeline will result in more career flexibility, increasing pathways, and reduction of risks.

GROUP: LIFE PRACTICES FRAMEWORK

D. ***Lifelong Learning and Skill Development*:** This variable examines and demonstrates the ability of an individual to keep current in the present career pathway while also pursuing skill attainment and development for future career moves. This will also have an impact on the length of an individual's career prospects (temporal window).

E. ***Physical Vibrancy*:** Physical vibrancy can impact both ability to keep existing jobs and ability to attract and attain new employment in case of job loss. It will also impact how long an individual's career (temporal window) can last.

F. ***Relational and Network Quality*:** Speaks to the quality of family and personal relationships and networks. These relationships (and the foundation they provide) can back up and support individuals in the event of personal and career disruption. This factor demonstrates an individual's ability to recognize and develop good support networks in both life and career.

GROUP: CAREER AND FINANCIAL PRACTICES FRAMEWORK

G. ***Risk Management (Abilities and Strategies)*:** This aspect of our measurement process deals with understanding of tools and strategies to manage both personal and career risks; this will relate to an individual's ability to endure/withstand adversity outside of that individual's direct control, both personally and professionally.

H. ***Financial Management and Planning Practices*:** An individual's understanding of sound financial practices and planning. These skills will provide a platform/ foundation to withstand personal and professional adversity.

I. ***Career Management*:** This component deals with how effective an individual is at managing and developing current career directions and future career prospects and pathways. This will impact the individual's ability to take care of current career outcomes and prospects as well as defining the correct directions and opportunities to pursue in the future.

APPENDIX C

Please Take the Promethean Measurement Test to Determine Your Convulsive Economic Quotient

http://larrystraub.com/

This self-scoring survey should take less than twenty minutes to take. It will provide your Convulsive Economic Quotient as well as recommendations on how to improve on any areas of weakness within your results.